Banks, Financial Development and Regional Growth

European University Studies
Europäische Hochschulschriften
Publications Universitaires Européennes

Series V
Economics and Management

Reihe V Série V
Volks- und Betriebswirtschaft
Sciences économiques, gestion d'entreprise

Vol./Bd. 3194

PETER LANG
Frankfurt am Main · Berlin · Bern · Bruxelles · New York · Oxford · Wien

Saovanee Chantapong

Banks, Financial Development and Regional Growth

Evidence from Thailand

PETER LANG
Europäischer Verlag der Wissenschaften

Bibliographic Information published by Die Deutsche Bibliothek
Die Deutsche Bibliothek lists this publication in the Deutsche Nationalbibliografie; detailed bibliographic data is available in the internet at <http://dnb.ddb.de>.

Zugl.: Hannover, Univ., Diss., 2005

D 89
ISSN 0531-7339
ISBN 3-631-54688-2
US-ISBN 0-8204-9831-9

www.peterlang.de

To my parents, sister and brothers

Contents

List of Figures

List of Tables

List of Abbreviations

BAAC	Bank for Agriculture and Agricultural Co-operatives
BIBFs	Bangkok International Banking Facilities
BIS	Bank for International Settlements
BOT	Bank of Thailand
CACs	Collective Action Clauses
CDRAC	Corporate Debt Restructuring Advisory Committee
EWSs	Early Warning Systems
FD	Financial Development
FIDF	Financial Institutions Development Fund
FRA	Financial Sector Restructuring Agency
FSAP	Financial Sector Assessment Program
FSIs	Financial Soundness Indicators
IBCA	International Bank Credit Analysis
ICOR	Incremental Capital Output Ratio
IFS	International Financial Statistics
IMF	International Monetary Fund
GDP	Gross Domestic Product
GMM	Generalised Method of Moments
GPP	Gross Provincial Product
NPLs	Non-performing Loans
NPV	Net Present Value
MLR	Minimum Lending Rate
MOR	Minimum Overdraft Rate
MRR	Minimum Retail Rate
OECD	Organisation for Economic Co-operation and Development
OLS	Ordinary Least Squares
ROA	Return on Asset
SET	Stock Exchange of Thailand
SFIs	Specialised Financial Institutions
TAMC	Thai Asset Management Corporation
UK	United Kingdom
US	United States
VAR	Vector Autoregression

Acknowledgements

I am deeply grateful to Professor Dr. Lukas Menkhoff, Chair, Money and International Finance Section at the University of Hannover, who was my first supervisor and Professor Dr. Thomas Lux, Chair, Department of Economics at the University of Kiel, who was my second supervisor for their valuable time and very helpful guidance and comments.

I first developed an interest in finance and banking and in the linkage between finance and economic growth when I worked at the Corporate Debt Restructuring Group, the Bank of Thailand (BOT) in the late 1990s, dealing with the corporate debt restructuring policies and the debt negotiation between the private sector and financial institutions with an aim to implement the debt restructuring process efficiently. This work was done within the so-called Bangkok framework for corporate debt restructuring, which is a non-binding and non-statutory framework (an informal framework outside bankruptcy proceedings), adopted for complicated corporate debt workouts involving multiple creditors, designed to promote timely co-operation amongst concerned stakeholders for their mutual benefit and based on general market acceptance. At its peak, the BOT's Corporate Debt Restructuring Advisory Committee (CDRAC) was advising on deals worth almost 50 percent of GDP. My work at that time provided me with valuable first-hand and in-depth insights into the causes of the 1997 Thai twin crisis, into how it affected financial institutions and corporations and into the linkages between financial and real sectors.

I started my research work relating to these issues at the Advanced Studies Programme in International Economic Policy Research (ASP), The Kiel Institute for World Economics (IFW), Kiel, in 2001-2002. I am very grateful to Prof. Dr. Harmen Lehment, Prof. Dr. Claudia Buch, Dr. Ralph P. Heinrich and Felix Hammermann for their helpful discussions and interchanges.

Out of this grew my Ph.D. research, which would not have been possible without support from many colleagues at the BOT. I thank Angsupalee Wacharakiat, Bussaracum Petchclai, Nuannute Thana-Anekcharoen, Dr. Panita Piya-oui, Somchai Lertlarpwasin and Supatpong Navaratana from BOT Headquarters and Nawaporn Maharagkaga, BOT's representative in London for helpful discussions and suggestions. I thank Prangtip Busayasiri, Chalalai Jiwasukapimat, and staff of the Data Management Department, BOT Headquarters, as well as Varintorn Chaivivat, BOT Northern Region Office, Amornrat Chamnong and Usanee Prechom, BOT Southern Region Office for providing the data and helping me with assembling the data and clarifying data issues. I also thank the Information Technology Office, the Comptroller General's Department, Ministry of Finance, the Statistical Forecasting Bureau, the National Statistical Office, Ministry of Information and Communication

Technology, and the National Economic and Social Development Board, the Office of the Prime Minister.

During the research I received valuable advice on econometrics from Dr. Stefan Niermann and Dr. Ralph P. Heinrich. The final study benefited from many detailed comments I received on earlier drafts, including Christian Heins, Daniela Beckmann, Felix Hammermann, Konrad Richter, and Raihan Zamil and participants of various conferences: the West-East Conference 'Accounting and Finance in Transition: European and Asian Experience and Public Policy Considerations, 10-12 July 2003, the Greenwich Business School, London; the Comparative Analysis of Enterprise (micro) Data Conference 2003, 15-16 September 2003, Cass Business School, London; the International Conference on Emerging Markets and Global Risk Management, 11-12 June 2004, the Westminster Business School, London; 7 Göttinger Workshop `Internationale Wirtschaftsbeziehungen´, 7-9 April 2005, Center for Globalisation and Europeanization of the Economy, Göttingen; the Xth Spring Meeting of Young Economists, 22-24 April 2005, Graduate Institute of International Studies (HEI), Geneva and the Annual Conference 2005 Verein für Socialpolitik Research Committee Development Economics, 8-9 July 2005, the Kiel Institute for World Economics (IFW), Kiel.

My utmost thanks go to Dr. Ralph P. Heinrich for many very helpful comments and suggestions and for patiently and thoroughly proof-reading earlier versions of the manuscript. I am very grateful to Christoph Ehlert, who has the gift for everything related to computers, for his great help in preparing all graphics and manuscripts.

I thank the ASP's alumni for financial support when I participated in the Advanced Studies Programme in International Economic Policy Research. I thank the Money and International Finance Section, Department of Economics, Faculty of Economics and Management, University of Hannover for financial support and for providing me with a friendly and good environment during the whole period of my research. My appreciation goes to the Bank of Thailand for granting me a temporary leave to pursue my research.

Specially, my true-hearted thanks go to Hirunya Chantapong, my sister for her great and continued support, Angsupalee Wacharakiat for her tremendous support as coordinator between the BOT and myself for the whole period of my study in Germany, Daniela Beckmann for her great help which made my days in Hannover breezy, Dr. Chuah Kim, Saichol Udomsin and Dr. Siriporn Tanodekeaw, my long-life friends from Manchester University, Brigitte Scholz, Felix Hammermann and Dr. Ralph P. Heinrich for their warm encouragements. The findings, interpretations, and conclusions expressed in this study are entirely mine. They do not necessarily reflect the opinion of the Bank of Thailand. Remaining errors are under my responsibility.

Hannover, Germany, September 2005

Saovanee Chantapong

Chapter 1 Introduction

Before the 1997 financial crisis, East Asian countries were acclaimed as being economic 'miracles'. In fact, regional economic growth during the 1960-95 periods had outpaced growth in other groups of developing countries (Grier, 2003). The onset and spread of the Asian economic and financial crisis revealed economic and political problems in the region and slowed down its growth to a certain extent. The International Monetary Fund (IMF) intervened with rescue packages in the magnitude of US$ 17 billion for Thailand, US$ 33 billion for Indonesia and US$ 57 billion for South Korea. However, most countries in the region rebounded from the financial crisis and experienced strong economic growth in recent years (Grier, 2003 and Rahman et al., 2004).

Twin crises, of which the 1997 Asian crises are examples, are the association of banking and currency crises. The well-known explanation of Asian banking crises consists of moral hazard problems in banking associated with rapid financial liberalisation and government deposit insurance, and large macroeconomic shocks (Glick and Hutchison, 1999). In addition, financial sectors were inefficiently supervised and regulated resulting in banking institutions accumulating large amounts of non-performing loans (NPLs) (Corsetti et al., 1998a and Rahman et al., 2004). As for the currency crises, in a more recent view crises were caused not only by a conflict between deteriorating fundamentals and the pegged exchange rate, but also by self-fulfilling prophecies (Obstfeld, 1994).

Bankers, economists and regulators generally agree that bank runs or failures are costly to the economy. If the problems in the banking sector are severe, the crisis will rapidly spread to the rest of the national financial system and possibly spread over the borders. Banking/financial crises can lead to currency crises if speculators anticipate that the authorities will choose inflation over exchange rate stability in order to avoid bankruptcies in the banking sector where banks hold high proportions of foreign debt in banks' balance sheets. In order to stop the capital flight and to defend the national currency, the central bank often raises interest rates. This in turn accelerates the domestic banking crisis. At the same time, if the national currency is depreciated, it will increase the value of the high proportion of foreign debt in the banking sector. The crises are followed by economic contraction, decreasing production and real incomes and increasing unemployment (Hölscher, 2000). Cross-country studies since the 1980s suggest that output losses during banking crises have been on average large, about over 10 percent of annual GDP[1]. The losses from banking crises in

[1] Argentina's banking crisis in the early 1980s (crisis period: 1980-1982) was the most expensive restructuring exercise, amounting to 55.1% of GDP, followed by Indonesia (crisis period: 1997-2002, fiscal outlay: 55.0% of GDP), Chile (1981-1983, 42.0% of GDP),

the developing countries tended to be larger relative to GDP than those in industrial economies (Caprio and Klingebiel, 1996).

Table 1.1: Patterns of Systemic Banking Crises[2]

Country	Crisis year 1/	Fiscal Cost (% of GDP)	Peak NPL (% of Loan)	Real GDP Growth 2/	Change in Exchange Rate 3/	Peak in Real Interest Rates 4/	Decline in Real Assets Prices 5/
Czech Rep	1998	14.0	38	+0.4%	-3.1%	6.2%	-56.6%
Finland	1992	11.0	13	-4.6%	-5.5%	14.3%	-34.6%
Indonesia	1998	50.0	65-75	-15.4%	-57.5%	3.3%	-78.5%
Korea	1998	37.0	30-40	-10.6%	-28.8%	21.6%	-45.9%
Malaysia	1998	16.4	25-35	-12.7%	-13.9%	5.3%	-79.9%
Mexico	1995	19.3	29.8	-6.2%	-39.8%	24.7%	-53.3%
Philippines	1998	0.5	20	-0.8%	-13.0%	6.3%	-67.2%
Sweden	1992	4.0	18	-3.3%	+1.0%	79.2%	-6.8%
Thailand	1998	32.8	33	-5.4%	-13.7%	17.2%	-77.4%

Note: 1) Crisis year is the peak crisis year.

2) The real GDP growth variables equal the percentage change in real fourth-quarter GDP in the crisis year compared to real fourth-quarter GDP one year before the crisis year. CPI inflation is used to get the real growth in GDP. The growth in GDP is in terms of local currency. GDP data are from IFS (IMF). The inflation rate equals the percentage change in the CPI during the crisis year and is from IFS.

3) The change in the exchange rate equals the percentage change of the exchange rate versus the US dollar during the first quarter of the crisis year. An increase in the exchange rate indicates an appreciation. The exchange rate data are from IFS.

4) The real interest rate spike equals the peak in the real money market rate during the crisis year. The interest rate data are from IFS.

5) The real growth in asset prices variable is the largest drop on a monthly basis in the stock market index during the crisis year compared to the level of the stock market index in January of the year before the crisis year. The return is in local currency and corrected for inflation. The data for Finland, Mexico and Sweden come from the DataStream global market indices and for the other countries, data come from the IFC global market indices.

Source: Claessens et al., 2001

Thailand (1997-2002, 34.8 % of GDP), Uruguay (1981-1984, 31.2% of GDP), Korea (1997-2002, 28% of GDP), Côte d'Ivoire (1988-1991, 25% of GDP), Senegal (1988-1991, 17% of GDP), Hungary (1991-1995, 10% of GDP), Norway (1990-1993, 8.0 % of GDP) and New Zealand (1987-1990, 1.0% of GDP) (see Caprio and Klingebiel, 1996 and Claessens et al., 2004).

[2] A systemic crisis can be characterised as a situation with large-scale corporate and financial distress. Typically, a systemic crisis results from large shocks to foreign exchange and interest rates, and a general economic slowdown, the corporate and financial sectors experience a large number of defaults and difficulties to repay their contracts on time, and non-performing loans increase rapidly (Claessens et al., 2001).

Figure 1.1: Bank Insolvency since 1980

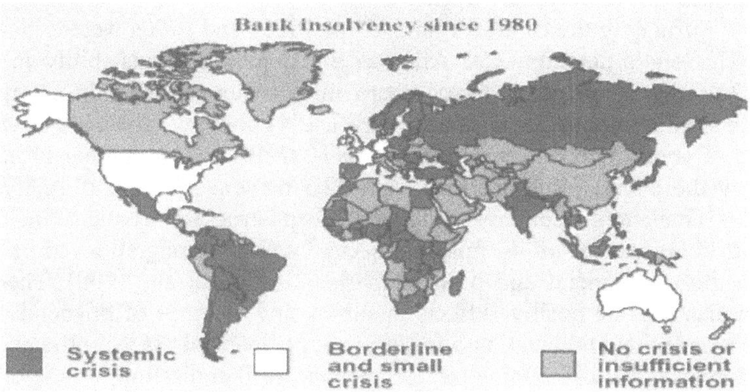

Source: Claessens, 1999

It is widely agreed that countries facing financial crises shared some features ranging from cronyism, over-borrowing, panic by foreign investors, liberalisation with inadequate regulation, boom and bust cycles and external economic shocks (Claessens, 1999). Table 1 shows some general characteristics of systemic financial crises in a sample of countries. Figure 1 shows countries which had bank insolvencies since 1980. Because systemic financial crises involve complicated coordination problems[3] associated with a lack of capital and the influence of the financial sector on economic growth, governments tend to take action in systemic restructuring, in particular in the banking sector. The main lesson from the study of crises between the late 1980s and early 1990s is that managing crises in emerging markets is much different from industrial countries because of the weaker financial institutions, larger degree of problems and different initial circumstances. Consequently, best practice from industrial countries cannot be simply applied to developing countries. Another lesson is that managing crises involves tradeoffs[4] between various policies, for example,

---

[3] The fortune of an individual firm or financial institution and the best course of action for its owners and managers depend on the actions of others and the general economic outlook (Claessens et al., 2004).

[4] Another potential trade-off is the one between maintaining financial stability today through intervention and future risks through increasing moral hazard later on. In practice, when individual banks face failures, the authorities have usually a preference to encourage a private sector solution where any losses are passed on to existing shareholders, managers and sometimes uninsured creditors, and not to the tax payers. However, most recent systemic crises have typically been caused by adverse macroeconomic shocks which make the whole financial system weak. In these situations, policy options seem to be limited. The private

containing fiscal costs, speeding up economic recovery and preventing a return of a crisis (Claessens et al., 2004).

Turning to the case of Thailand, the 1980s and 1990s were critical periods for Thailand's development. After an initial period of instability in the early 1980s[5], characterised by large macro imbalances resulting from rapid credit expansion and loose fiscal policy, Thailand's economy expanded at an average pace of about 9 percent per year during 1987-1996. The number of households below the poverty line dropped from 32.6 percent in 1988 to 16.3 percent in 1996. Thailand's economy underwent deep structural changes including the rapid liberalisation of its financial sector[6] and the integration of its economy with global financial and product markets[7] (Alba et al., 1999). The financial liberalisation had positive effects in stimulating the pace of financial deepening and broadening and creating a wider range of financial assets in the portfolios of the household and corporate sectors. Financial liberalisation, on the other hand, made the task of monetary management more complex[8] with a low degree of central bank autonomy (Sirivedhin, 1998).

Banks in emerging economies normally are weaker than those in industrialised countries, in terms of capital base, performance and regulations. But it is unlikely that they are inefficient in resource management (Bhagwati, 2002 and Menkhoff and Suwanaporn, 2003). Menkhoff and Suwanaporn (2003) found that Thai banks have not performed worse than banks in other countries, both in terms of allocative and operational efficiency. However, it seems that a large number of Thai financial institutions were distressed by the first half of 1997. What happened in the Thai banking sector? What made the favourable

---

sector solution seems difficult. Consequently, foreign takeover and government intervention are needed (Hoggarath et al., 2004).

[5] In response to this instability, Thailand implemented a macro stabilisation programme during the period 1984-87. The programme included a large devaluation of the nominal exchange rate in late 1984 with tighter fiscal policies. The Baht was devalued about 15 percent in nominal effective terms and then pegged against an undisclosed basket that weighted heavily the US Dollar (see Alba et al., 1999).

[6] See details of major financial liberalisation and reforms since in the mid-1980s in Sirivedhin (1998).

[7] With reference to World Bank (1997 cited in Alba et al., 1999), Thailand moved from a country partially integrated between 1985-87 to one of the most integrated emerging market economies between 1992 and 1994, In this period Thailand experienced very large and sustained foreign capital inflows, with an average of 9.4 percent of GDP per year during 1988-96.

[8] For example, it is inadequate to monitor only commercial banks' credits during the increasing popularity of direct financing and foreign borrowing. Domestic interest rates have become a major channel of monetary transmission; nevertheless, they are much affected by foreign interest rates. The inter-bank rate shock seems to have no effect on private investment. Also, the wealth effects are likely to have a strong effect on household saving behaviour and the monetary policy management needs to be taken it into account (Sirivedhin, 1998).

performance disappear within a few years? What are the consequences of the 1997 Thai crisis for the banking sector? What are the policy implications? What can we do to prevent financial crises in the future? Did banks in Asian countries perform as well as those of developed countries? In the aftermath of the 1997 Thai financial crisis, there was also observable evidence that the impact of monetary policy[9] on output has weakened since 1999, and that this has partly resulted from a weaker bank-lending channel (Disyatat and Vongsinsirikul, 2003). These findings raise the question whether financial development and the associated changes in the banking industry contributed to the economic performance or whether causality ran from economic performance to financial development. A related question is whether there are long-run effects of financial development on economic growth.

This dissertation is intended to answer those questions. Although this study is based on the case of Thailand, international evidence and comparisons are also included. The dissertation includes four main chapters. Following these introductory remarks, some theoretical issues relating to financial structure and economic development are discussed. Chapter 2 provides a policy-oriented survey on the 1997 Thai crisis and its consequences for the banking sector. It gives an overview of the causes of the Thai twin crisis, exploring both macroeconomic imbalances and microeconomic distortions in the financial sector. The policies undertaken to manage the crisis which aimed at getting the macroeconomic policies right, strengthening financial systems, improving governance and transparency and modernising the legal and regulatory environment are discussed. This is followed by the consequences for the banking sector and for financial intermediation. For example, banks have returned to profitability since 2001, but the large overhang of NPLs has not been fully solved. This has made the credit channel less effective in the transmission of monetary policy. Some lessons from the crisis are explored, focusing on the one hand on how to solve a crisis once it occurs (with emphasis on the closure of nonviable financial companies and bank and corporate debt restructuring, which need clear and orderly procedures in order to minimise costs), and on the other hand on how to prevent crises in the future.

Chapter 3 presents an empirical study of cost efficiency of domestic and foreign banks in Thailand. The study estimates and compares cost efficiency of domestic and foreign banks in Thailand by using bank-panel data between 1995 and 2003. It also examines the effect of foreign bank entry on banking efficiency in Thailand since the significant acquisitions by foreign banks after the 1997 financial crisis. The widely used translog functional form specification is

---

[9] Monetary transmission channels can be divided into five different channels: direct monetary transmission, interest rate channel, asset price channel, credit channel and expectations and uncertainty (see also figure 1.A.1: Monetary transmission channels in Bondt, 2000).

statistically tested by pooled regressions. The estimated results suggest that the unit costs of production of domestic and foreign banks are indistinguishable, although the two types of banks focus on different areas of the banking business. The findings suggest that based on bank operating efficiency, if foreign banks represent the best-practice banks in the industry, to a large extent, domestic banks in Thailand have caught up to the best-practice standards throughout 1995-2003. The unit costs of production of domestic banks after the foreign bank entry through acquisitions declined, suggesting that the cost efficiency of domestic banks improved. This may be due to greater foreign participation through acquisitions, which increases the competitive pressure in the banking industry, and also to financial restructuring of domestic banks, which increases the cost efficiency of domestic banks, thereby benefiting banking customers.

Chapter 4 presents an empirical study of the dynamic relationship between financial development and economic growth from a regional perspective. There are many cross-country studies relating to the relationship between growth and financial development; however, there is less evidence on the effect of local financial development within the regions of a single country. This chapter is intended to fill this gap. Advantages of examining the relationship between finance and growth in a regional perspective within a single country are as follows: the region represents a more accurate definition of the relevant retail bank market and all related institutional, legal and cultural factors are likely to be constant across regions within a country, thereby ensuring that differences in economic performance across regions are not driven by those factors. The chapter also investigates the causality between economic development and financial development. It finds that the growth rates of real gross provincial product (GPP) per capita for 23 years between 1981 and 2003 are significantly negatively related to the initial level of real GPP per capita (1981) as expected from absolute convergence in growth theory. With reference to the concept of conditional convergence, the results show that there is divergence of real GPP per capita/worker in Thailand during 1994-2003, suggesting that among provinces with the same financial development, the richer ones grew faster. However, when the initial level of real GPP per capita/worker is held constant, neither credits nor branches robustly correlated with growth. Based on the Granger causality test results, there is a bi-directional causality between finance and growth. Chapter 5 summarises the main findings and policy implications.

Figure 1.A.1: Monetary Transmission Channels

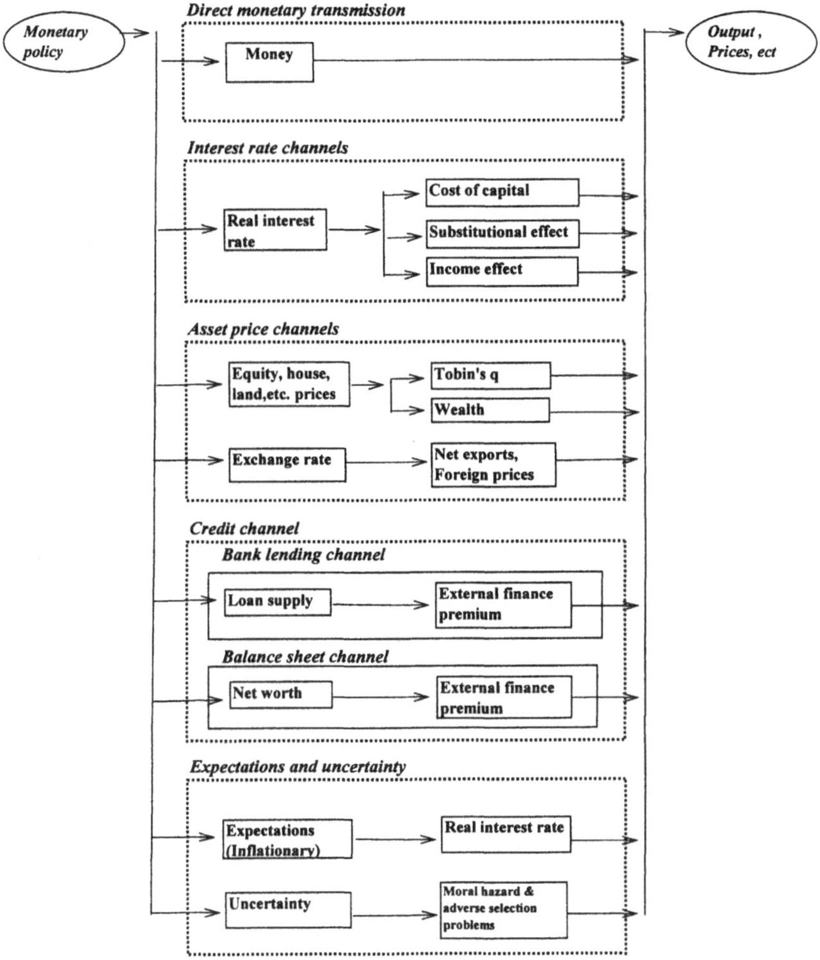

Source: Bondt, 2000

Chapter 2 Policy Oriented Survey on the 1997 Thai Crisis: Description and Consequences for the Banking Sector

For historians each event is unique. Economics, however, maintains that forces in society and nature behave in repetitive ways. History is particular; economics is general.
(Charles Kindelberger, 1978, qtd. in Kaminsky and Reinhart, 1999).

2.1 Introduction

Notwithstanding a strong reserve position and macroeconomic performance between mid 1980s and mid-1990s, The Thai baht came under speculative pressure in early 1995. Speculative prove short-lived, nevertheless, the authorities intervened to keep the peg in place. Stock price, measured in dollars, remained unaffected by the events in Mexico and elsewhere. After a slight decrease, the index began to recover. However, The Thai economy faced various difficulties in 1997, for example, the current account deficit remained very high, the country highly depended on short-term foreign capital which overly exposed to unproductive and speculative investment in the asset markets and the export competitiveness eroded. The economic problems significantly affected market confidence, leading to chronic currency speculative throughout the first half of 1997. The central bank intervened the Baht in the foreign exchange market; however, it was insufficient to regain the confidence in the Baht and foreign capital outflow continued. The problem of non-performing loans (NPLs) caused the loss of both creditors' and depositors' confidence in a number of finance companies (Radelet and Sachs, 1998).

The Thai economy in 1997 suffered a severe twin crisis that is a more or less simultaneous crisis in the balance of payments and in the banking system. A series of speculative attacks on the Thai bath depleted the nation's currency reserves and sent short-term interest rates (overnight inter-bank rate) to 21.7 percent. On July, 2 1997 the authorities abandoned the exchange rate peg relative to a basket of currencies and allowed the bath to float. As a result the currency plunged by 17.4 percent in nominal terms and by an additional 58.3 percent in the following six months and by an additional 91.3 percent at a peak in January 1998.

On the financial account of the balance of payments, capital inflows, which had averaged 14.4 billions of U.S. dollars in the preceding five years (1992-1996), dried up, and Thailand suffered capital outflows of an average of 7.4 billions of US. Dollar in the post-crisis years (1997 to 2001). Similarly, the current account balance which had been in deficit to the tune of 7.9 percent of GDP in 1996 before the crisis, turned sharply into surplus of 12.7 and 10.2 percent of GDP in 1998 and 1999. As a result of the crisis, real GDP contracted by 1.4 percent in 1997 and 10.5 percent in 1998. Unemployment rate rose from 1.5 percent of the labour force in 1996 before the crisis to a peak of 4.4 percent in 1998. At the same time, non-performing loans in the banking sector rose rapidly about 45.0 percent of total loans at end-1998, and a series of finance companies and commercial banks got into trouble. In the event, 69 finance companies and 7 commercial banks had to be closed, merged or temporarily taken over by the authorities. Since then, the economy has started to grow again, as interest rates returned to more normal levels, the exchange rate stabilized and foreign capital returned. The banking sector has improved its balance sheet considerably. However, non-performing loans continue to be a problem.

In the following second section, the present paper gives an overview of the causes of the Thai twin crisis, exploring both macroeconomic imbalances and microeconomic distortions in the financial sector. The third section discusses the policies undertaken to manage the crisis which aim at getting the macroeconomic policies right, strengthening financial systems, improving governance and transparency and modernising the legal and regulatory environment. The fourth section looks at the consequences for the banking sector and for financial intermediation, for example, banks' balance sheets have returned to profitability since 2001, however, a large overhang of NPLs has not been fully solved. This has led the credit channel less effective as the monetary policy transmission. The fifth section explores some lessons from the crisis, focusing on the one hand on how to solve a crisis once it occurs which emphasises on the strategies in the closure of nonviable financial companies and bank and corporate debt restructuring which need clear and sequence procedures with minimised costs, and on the other hand on how to prevent crises in the future. The country which wants to prevent itself from the future crisis or minimise loss when a crisis occurs should create efficient early warning system, combined with standard country surveillance, reduce vulnerability of its economy by getting macroeconomic policies right and by ensuring sound banking, increasing international liquidity and shifting toward risk-based incentives to supervision regulations and establish a new economic institution with an aim of deepening economic cooperation within the region. The sixth section concludes.

2.2 What caused the Asian Crises?

The question raised by then Deputy Treasury Secretary Lawrence Summers to one of the authors at the height of the Asian crisis was that 'you study history. Can you tell us, whether the crisis problem is growing more severe (Bordo and Eichengreen, 2002)? As a response to this question, section 2 explores various economic literatures relating to the evolution of financial crises. To what extent can they make us understand the causes and symptoms of the Asian crises? Did the crisis problem become more severe than before?

2.2.1 Theories relating to Asian Twin Crises

The leading explanations of Asian banking crises include the well-known 'moral hazard' problems in banking associated with financial liberalisation and government deposit insurance, and large macroeconomic shocks, for example, a sudden decrease in underlying asset values (Glick and Hutchinson, 1999). Also, the Asian banking and financial systems were fragile both in terms of inefficient supervision and regulation, and these conditions were observed even before the onset of the crisis (Corsetti et al., 1998a).

The classical view of currency crises is that pegged exchange rates can exist as long as monetary authorities are credibly committed to maintaining them. Internal economic policy should be compatible with the objective of maintaining the fixed exchange rate. When there is the incompatibility of the pegged exchange rate and expansionary domestic financial policy, speculative attacks on a currency may occur (Bordo and Schwartz, 2000). In addition, countries can face currency crises if competitive trends have changed the real exchange rate which actually requires adjustment of the nominal parity. However, countries may resist adjusting their parities because of the effect of adverse capital movement. At the end of day, parity adjustment is compelled; it will be traumatic (Bordo and Schwartz, 2000).

However, in a more recent view, currency crises are driven not only by a conflict between deteriorating fundamentals and the pegged exchange rate, but also by self-fulfilling prophecies (Obstfeld, 1994). Unlike the classical view, in the more recent view the timing of the attack is difficult to predict. What matters to speculators is the trade-off between domestic and external goals of monetary authorities and how authorities will react when they face a crisis. A crisis can occur in multiple equilibria and indeterminacy in foreign exchange markets (Bordo and Schwartz, 2000). The 1992 EMS crisis is cited as an example of a currency crisis unlikely to be related to the behaviour of fundamentals. The explanation of this is the presence of multiple equilibria in foreign exchange markets which can be triggered by random shocks like sunspots (Bordo and Schwartz, 1996, p.6). Some well-known historical examples of currency crises ranging from John Law's operation, 1716-20, Mexican devaluation, 1976, 1982, 1994 to the crisis in the European Exchange Rate Mechanism, 1992-93 (see Bordo and Schwartz, 1996 and appendix 2.A.2).

As for the twin crises which are the apparent case of the 1997 Asian crises, in theory (see table 2.A.1.1), Glick and Hutchison (1999) pointed out that the twin crises which are the association of bank and currency crises may be attributable to three main channels of causation. The first causality is a banking crisis leading to a currency crisis. A weak banking sector may suddenly lead to a currency crisis if speculators anticipate that the authorities will choose inflation over exchange rate stability in order to avoid bankruptcies on the banking sector rather than endure the costs of defending the domestic currency (Obstfeld,

1994). The governments should explicitly consider devalue their local currency as one of the logical policy options to confront a bank run problem in a fixed exchange rate regime. Then, what causes a banking crisis? The well-known explanations are moral hazard problems in banking associated with financial liberalisation and government deposit insurance, and large macroeconomic shocks, for example a sharp decrease in underlying asset values (e.g. bubble crash in asset prices). An alternative explanation relating possibly non-fundamental factor is that bank runs may occur because of the individual depositors and creditors expectations (Glick and Hutchison, 1999).

The second causality is a currency crisis leading to a banking crisis. Obstfeld (1994) pointed out that a currency crisis my lead to a vulnerable banking sector if policy-makers respond to the pressure on the exchange rate by significantly raising interest rates. In addition, banks can be vulnerable due to large un-hedged foreign liabilities and/or a maturity mismatch between assets and liabilities. In short, a currency crisis shock can lead to banking sector distress both directly by causing a deterioration of bank balance sheets if the currency is allowed to depreciate, or indirectly by causing the central bank to raise interest rates to defend the local currency.

The third causality is joint causality where financial liberalisation is combined with moral hazard incentives that induce banks to invest in risky portfolios, including un-hedged foreign currency liabilities. At the same time deposit insurance may fuel a lending boom involving both foreign and domestic credit expansion that finally leads to a banking and currency crisis (Glick and Hutchison, 1999). Deterioration in banks' net worth, caused by exchange rate changes, reduces the ability to pay back foreign debt and raises the cost of funds from abroad. In turn, the adverse shocks in terms of a decline in the expected return on domestic lending and an increase in non-performing loans or an increase in government deficit could lead to a foreign exchange crisis (Buch and Heinrich, 1999).

In fact, there is a close link between a country's currency stability and the health of its banking sector. Devaluation worsens the balance sheets of financial intermediaries which lead to a pronounced tightening in credit market conditions and possibly lead to a contraction in output. The adverse consequences of a devaluation are even worse if banks' balance sheets are deteriorated by non-performing loans (NPLs), or if banks borrow heavily in foreign currencies at short horizons. Banking and currency crises can amplify each other and generate a vicious circle (Pesenti and Tille, 2000).

Krugman (1999) stated that the first and second generation models[1] are

[1] First generation models explaining currency crises like that in Mexico 1973 and 1982, second generation models which lead to multiple equilibriums and twin crises which occurred after the financial liberalisation since 1980s (Krugman, 1979 and Obstfeld, 1994). The

considerably related to particular financial crises of the 1990s. For example, the Russian crisis of 1998 was driven by the weak government which was about to be forced to finance itself by the printing press, whereas the sterling crisis of 1992 was driven by the perception that the UK government needed to choose between domestic employment and exchange rate stability. Thus, Krugman (1999) constructed another candidate for the third generation crisis modelling which is designed to make sense of the number and nature of the emerging market crises of 1997-1998. It focuses on two facts which have not been mentioned in the formal models: the role of companies' balance sheets in determining their ability to invest and that of capital flows in affecting the real exchange rate. The factors that make financial collapse possible are as follows: high leverage of entrepreneurs and large foreign-currency debt relative to exports. These factors make the circular dynamics from investment to real exchange rate to balance sheets to investment more powerful. In sum, he stresses that extensive borrowing denominated in foreign currencies made Asian economies peculiarly vulnerable to financial collapse if the real exchange rate depreciated (Krugman, 1999, p. 468-469).

In the 1990s, some studies (for example: Saqib, 2002 and Kaminsky and Reinhart, 2003) of the recent Mexican crisis in 1994-95 and the East Asian crises in 1997-98 have focused also on some non-conventional determinants. First is the notion of market euphoria which says that most of the crises in recent times did not result from a darkening of economic conditions. In contrast, they

---

explanations of the first generation models of the collapse of fixed exchange rates which are based on fundamentals include overvalued real exchange rates and other macroeconomic factors, for example, budget deficits, and rapid credit expansion. A currency peg must be abandoned once the nation's foreign exchange reserves run out (Allen and Gale, 2003). However, Obstfeld (1994) pointed out that one cannot fully understand European currency experience in 1992-93 in terms of the first generation model. For industrial European countries with access to world capital markets, reserve adequacy is unlikely to be a concern today, unlike it was in the early 1970s when capital accounts had not yet been liberalised. Importantly, high interest rates and an increase in unemployment played an active role in determining how different governments responded to the 1992-93 crises. In this regard, the possibility of self-fulfilling crises cannot be easily dismissed. Speculative anticipations depend on conjectured government responses. At the same time, government responses also depend on price changes, which are fuelled by expectations of the government's economic and political position. The circular relationship implies that whether a potential crisis does or does not occur depends on whether market participants expect them to. In short, the second generation models which are based on non-fundamentals focus on the existence of multiple equilibria and self-fulfilling speculative attacks that can occur when the policymakers are willing to give up a pegged exchange rate if output and employment costs exceed a certain threshold (Glick and Hutchison, 1999).

occurred after a prolonged period of high economic growth. Second is the problem of contagion. The Asian crises, like the European Exchange Rate Mechanism and Tequilla crises, tended to spread among countries due to informational cascades (herding behaviour contagion), due to similar macroeconomic fundamentals (fundamental contagion), due to trade or political proximity (real integration or political contagion) and due to third-country investors who balanced their portfolios in other countries to cover crisis-induced losses from the triggering country (institutional contagion). Third are political factors that delay the implementation of a stabilisation programme or policy reform. Many governments have repeatedly failed to undertake the required devaluations and/or shrewd monetary or fiscal policies. (Saqib, 2002).

In addition, Corsetti et al., (2001b) studied the role of large players in currency crises in the 1990s[2] from different models of speculative attacks. They suggested that the presence of large traders and other highly leveraged institutions such as hedge funds can increase a country's vulnerability to a crisis because it makes other investors more aggressive in their position-taking in the sense that they choose to liquidate their currency positions despite strong economic fundamentals, compared to the case without large investors. Basically, because of her arbitrarily well-quality of information, the large trader will always attack the currency, using the full amount of the resources given to her. Thus, the overall amount of resources in the market increases. As a result, in the presence of a large trader, the region of the fundamentals where the currency is expected to collapse seems wider, then, the small agents are willing to follow a more aggressive trading strategy. It should be noted that the key assumption that the large trader profits in the event of devaluation may not always be the case. In addition, some unorthodox policy actions, for instance, the massive Hong Kong intervention in its equity market and capital controls in Malaysia could squeeze on the speculative short positions of highly leveraged institutions.

2.2.2 Evidence of the Asian Twin Crises and the 1997 Thai Twin Crisis

2.2.2.1 Evidence of the Asian Twin Crises

In principle, international financial integration should help countries to reduce macroeconomic volatility. However, the process of capital account liberalisation seems to have been accompanied by increased vulnerability to crises. Cross-country financial linkages amplify effects of various shocks and transmit them fast across national borders. Crises can be regarded as dramatic episodes of volatility. The phenomenon of financial and currency crises among developing

---

[2] The examples of case studies include the Thai baht crisis, the double play on the Hong Kong stock and foreign exchange markets in 1998, the Malaysian ringgit in 1997-98 and the pressures on the Australian dollar in June and August 1998 (Corsetti et al., 2001b, p. 38-47).

economies is frequently viewed as a natural consequence of the 'growing pains' associated with financial globalisation (Prasad et al., 2003).

The roots of the Asian currency and financial crises reflected a complex web of structural distortions and fundamental weaknesses in the countries of the region as summarised in the following (Corsetti et al., 1998a, 1998b and 1998c, Radelet and Sachs, 1998, and Lamfalussy, 2000):
1) Current account imbalance problem: Most Asian countries that faced currency attacks in 1997 experienced large and persistent current account deficits throughout the 1990s:
2) Sustainability problem: High growth rates may induce overly optimistic beliefs that the economic expansion will persist sustainable in the future. However, an external shock that leads to a rapid change in expectations can cause a sudden reversal of capital flows and produce unexpected depreciation of the currency;
3) Investment efficiency problem: Unlike the Latin American countries that experienced currency and financial crises in the recent years, the Asian countries were characterised by very high rates of investment throughout the 1990s. The ICORs (Incremental Capital Output Ratios) of most of Asian countries had increased rapidly in the 1993-1996 period, compared to those in the 1987-1992;
4) Significant real exchange rate appreciation: All Asian currencies that crashed in 1997 had experienced a real appreciation. Countries with appreciating currencies normally experienced a large deterioration of the current account;
5) Imbalances of foreign debt accumulation and management: A large proportion of a country's external debt was short-term and a crisis may take the form of a pure liquidity shortfall when panicking occurs; and
6) Inappropriate foreign exchange reserves: In most Asian countries the ratio of M2 to foreign reserves was relatively high in 1996-1997.

Glick and Hutchison (1999) investigated the causal linkage between bank and currency crises[3] by using a broad country and time-series data set including 90 industrial and developing countries between 1975 and 1997 as shown in table 2.A.1.2 The data set includes observations with and without crises which allow the authors to draw more general conclusions about the conditions that distinguish crisis from normal periods both across countries and across time. A total of 90 banking crisis episodes, 202 currency crises, and 37 twin crises were included. They found that only in emerging market economies, banking crises predict currency crises; however, currencies crises do not seem to be a particularly good leading indicator of the onset of future banking crises. The recent financial liberalisation is the most powerful single predictor of banking

[3] Arteta and Eichengreen (2001) is a good summary of the literature on emerging market twin crises.

sector problems. The relative frequency of individual banking and twin crises can be seen in table 2.1 illustrating that individual banking and currency crises

Table 2.1: Bank and Currency Crises

Time Distribution	1975-97	1975-79	1980-84	1985-89	1990-94	1995-97
Bank Crises						
Number	90	6	16	21	30	17
Frequency 1/	5.0	1.6	4.2	5.3	7.2	6.8
Currency Crises						
Number	202	39	45	50	48	20
Frequency 1/	11.3	11.0	12.0	12.6	11.6	8.0
Twin Crises						
Number	37	3	5	8	11	10
Frequency 1/	2.1	0.8	1.3	2.0	2.6	4.0

Developmental and Geographic distribution				Developing			
	Industrial	Develop-ing	Emerging	Africa	Asia	Latin America	Others 2/
Bank Crises							
Number	19	71	46	21	15	26	9
Frequency 1/	4.4	5.2	6.6	5.8	5.0	5.1	4.8
Currency Crises							
Number	42	160	78	59	29	53	19
Frequency 1/	9.6	11.8	11.2	16.5	9.6	10.4	10.2
Twin Crises							
Number	7	30	23	11	7	8	4
Frequency 1/	1.6	2.2	3.3	3.1	2.3	1.6	2.2

Source: Glick and Hutchison, 1999, p.29

Note: Twin crises are defined as banking crises accompanied by a currency crisis in previous, current, or following year.

1/ Number of crises divided by total sum of country-years.

2/ Including Eastern Europe and the Middle East.

as well as twin crises have been more frequent in developing and emerging markets than in industrial countries. Banking and twin crises have been notably evident in emerging markets.

Unlike Glick and Hutchison's work, Kaminsky and Reinhart (1999) restricted their data set to a limited number of countries experiencing crises. They constructed a chronology of events in the banking and external sectors and drew conclusions about the possible causal patterns among banking and balance of payments problems and financial liberalisation. They also studied the behaviour of macroeconomic indicators around the crisis periods. Their main results are very similar to Glick and Hutchison's work: Firstly, in the 1980s, after the financial liberalisation across many parts of the world, banking and currency crises become closely linked. Bhagwati (2002) holds the similar point of view that financial liberalisation was hasty and did not pay sufficient attention to the fact that the capital market is not as safe as good markets, and it needs to be monitored and regulated prudently. Frequently, the occurrence of banking sector problems predicts the balance of payment crisis. The existing banking sector problems were aggravated or new ones created by the high interest rates required to defend the exchange rate peg or the foreign exchange exposure of banks.

Table 2.2: The Onset of Financial Crises: Early Signals

Indicators	Percent of crises Accurately Called					
	Balance of Payments Crises					Banking Crises
	Total	Single	Twin	Before Financial Liberalisation	After Financial Liberalisation	
Financial Sector	67	67	67	67	68	65
Financial Liberalisation	74	72	78	64	77	71
M2 Multiplier	76	75	78	74	77	73
Domestic Credit/GDP	61	59	67	56	65	50
Real Interest Rate	89	86	94	78	91	100
Lending-Deposit Rate Ratio	71	70	73	50	73	57
Others	57	58	53	57	56	57
Excess M1 Balance	37	43	22	52	26	32
M2/Reserves	81	79	89	74	86	75
Bank Deposits	51	52	47	44	56	67
External Sector	72	71	74	72	72	82
Current Account	68	67	70	70	66	75
Exports	85	83	89	78	89	88
Terms of Trade	75	72	83	73	77	96
Real Exchange Rate	59	57	67	58	60	58
Imports	52	57	39	73	40	60
Capital Account	81	80	83	74	83	96
Reserves	75	74	79	70	78	92
Real Interest Rate Differential	86	86	88	78	89	100
Real Sector	69	69	70	61	72	85
Output	74	73	77	68	76	89
Stock Prices	64	65	63	53	68	81
Fiscal Sector	28	27	29	21	31	44

Source: Kaminsky and Reinhart: 1999

Notes: Episodes in which the beginning of a banking crisis is followed by a balance-of-payments crisis within 48 months are classified as twin crises. An indicator is said to have accurately called a crisis if it issues at least one signal in the crisis window on the basis of the criterion shown in Table 2.A.1.3 For each indicator, each cell in the table represents the number of times that indicator correctly calls a crisis as a percentage of the total number of crises. For the different sectors, each cell represents the simple average of the percentage of crises accurately called by all the individual variables in that group.

Secondly, both types of crises have common causes. They are preceded by weak and deteriorating economic fundamentals (see details in table 2.2), such as recessions or slowdown economic growth partly attributed to worsening of the terms of trade, an overvalued exchange rate and rising cost of credits. Also, a financial shock from increased easy access to international capital markets activates a boom-bust cycle. So it seems unlikely that crises are self-fulfilling. Finally, when currency and banking crises occur jointly, they are more severe than when they occur separately (Kaminsky and Reinhart, 1999).

The Asian countries experienced very high rates of investment, accounting for between 30-40 percent of GDP during 1990s. With the exception of Korea, all the Asian currencies that devalued in 1997 had experienced a real appreciation. A large part of explanation of the real appreciation after 1995 in many Asian countries is the strengthening of the US dollar with which they pegged their currencies (Calvo and Reinhart, 2000). One of the main reasons why many Asian countries maintained a policy of effective peg against the US dollar was to facilitate external financing of domestic projects with a low currency risk premium. One blames fixed exchange rates[4] for severe 1997 financial crises, and these countries were advised to allow their currencies to float.

The Asian countries experienced strong currency and banking crises which caused severe contractions of real GDP. Barro's study (2001) focuses on the immediate and long-term effects of the Asian financial crisis on economic performance in East and Southeast Asia[5]. The study indicates that five East and Southeast Asian countries, namely, Indonesia, Malaysia, South Korea, the Philippines and Thailand, experienced a severe output loss, compared with their previous growth trends and with other East Asian countries that were less affected by the crises. In fact, in East and Southeast Asia, the twin crises reduced economic growth over a five-year period (1995-2000) about 2 percent per year, and by 3 percent for the 1997-1998 crisis years.

Why are countries reluctant to allow large fluctuation in their exchange rates? What is the suitable exchange rate regime? Calvo and Reinhart's (2000) study which is based on monthly data on exchange rate, nominal and real interest rates and money for 39 countries in Africa, Asia, Europe and the Western Hemisphere between January 1970 and April 1999 responds to these questions. They found that the mean probability that the exchange rate is contained inside a 2 ½ band is significantly different when comparing the fixed

---

[4] According to the IMF's classification scheme, countries can be grouped into four main types of exchange rate arrangements as follows: pegs, limited flexibility, managed floating and freely floating (Calvo and Reinhart, 2000, p. 11).

[5] In his study, the countries in the sample include China, Hong Kong, Indonesia, Japan, South Korea, Malaysia, the Philippines, Singapore, Taiwan and Thailand (Barro, 2001).

exchange rate regime with the freely floating; however, other differences across regimes seem to be blurred.

With respect to the volatility measurement of international reserves[6], the study found that based on a 2.5 percent band, reserve variability is highest for the floating exchange rate regime and least for the limited flexibility regime. In all, large fluctuations in foreign exchange reserves occur associated with a higher extent of intervention in the foreign exchange market which can be interpreted that these countries try to lean against the wind.

It is generally recognised that when policy makers have to make a choice between stabilising interest rates and stabilising exchange rates, they tend to choose to stabilise the exchange rate because exchange rate stabilisation provides the economy with a clear-cut nominal anchor (Calvo and Reinhart, 2000). The commodity prices in the local currency are more variable than the exchange rate and there is almost no correlation among the two. It seems likely that the exchange rate is not allowed to absorb the shocks as indicated in the text book (Calvo and Reinhart, 2000). Interestingly, the issue of `different exchange rate systems´ has been debated. Unfortunately, it will continue being an `endless debate´ (Bhagwati, 2002).

The multi-faceted evidence on the structure of incentives, in the context of regulatory inadequacies and close links between public and private institutions is at the root of the Asian twin crisis. Importantly, the moral hazard problem in Asia magnified the financial vulnerability of the region during the financial liberalisation process in the 1990s. The problem can be classified into three different interrelated dimensions at the corporate, financial, and international level.

At the corporate level, with financial and industry policy involved with a widespread business sector network of personal and political favouritism, and with governments that tended to be willing to intervene in favour of troubled firms, markets operated under the condition that the return on investment was to some extent insured against adverse shocks. At the financial level, a long list of structural distortions[7] in the pre-twin crisis period, ranging from lax supervision and weak regulation to non-market criteria of credit allocation, associated with the rapid process of capital account liberalisation and financial market deregulation during the 1990s caused the adverse consequences. At the

---

[6] The volatility measurement of international reserves is defined as probability that the monthly percent change in foreign exchange reserves falls within a +/- 2.5 percent band (Calvo and Reinhart, 2000, table 6-9).

[7] A long list of structural distortions includes lax supervision and weak regulation; low capital adequacy ratios; lack of incentive-compatible deposit insurance schemes; insufficient expertise in the regulatory institutions; distorted incentives for project selection and monitoring; corrupt lending practices; non-market criteria of credit allocation (Corsetti et al.,1998a).

international level, moral hazard behaviour can be linked to the behaviour of international banks. They presumed that cross-border liabilities, mostly in the form of short-term inter-bank loans would be fully guaranteed by either debtor governments or an indirect bail-out through an IMF rescue programme. In short, the core implication of moral hazard is that in the event of adverse shocks, the anticipation of a bail-out provides a strong incentive for financial intermediaries to take more risk (Corsetti et al., 1998a).

2.2.2.2 Evidence of the 1997 Thai Twin Crisis

From macroeconomic, external and banking data shown in table 2.A.1.4, it can be concluded that Thailand experienced large and persistent current account imbalances[8]. The current account deficit in Thailand stood over 6.0 percent of GDP during the 1990s and stood at about 8.0 in 1996, one of the highest anywhere in the world. In addition, the resource balance gap of Thailand in 1996 was quite large, accounting for 6.9 percent of GDP (see a summary of the calculation in appendix 2.A.3). The assessment of the current account deficits depends on the sustainability[9] of external balances. Sometimes, the notion of sustainability is problematic. For example, creditors are willing to lend according to their assumptions in the solvency criterion but for some circumstances, foreign creditors suddenly change their perception of the risk that the country would renege to its liabilities. Then, creditors require a higher default premium or stop giving their loans (Corsetti et al., 1998a and Feldstein, 1999).

Thailand had its currency pegged to a basket of currencies, of which the dollar was a large component. Thailand's investment rates stood at more than 40 percent of GDP during the same period. However, with a measure of investment efficiency by using ICOR[10], Thailand's ICOR increased from in an average of 3.4 percent during 1987-1992 to 5.1 percent during 1993-1996. It is indicated that the investment efficiency showed the declining trend before the 1997 crisis year (Corsetti et al., 1998a).

As for the contagion issue, based on information from newspapers on the key world events associated with significant stock price changes, Kaminsky and Reinhart (2003) found that financial shocks often traverse to other countries.

---

[8] Data on the current account positions provide some preliminary evidence in the sense that the currency crises may link to an external competitiveness problem. In fact, with taking 1990 as the base year, by the spring of 1997, the real exchange rate of currencies of high-deficit countries, i.e. Thailand, Malaysia, Philippines, and Indonesia appreciated by 12%, 19%, 23%, and 8% respectively (Corsetti et al., 1998a).

[9] The meaning of sustainability in this context considers that a country running a current account deficit and accumulating foreign debt relative to its GDP so as to be solvent, the country requires run trade surpluses at some point in the future (Corsetti et al., 1998a).

[10] Incremental capital output ratio (ICOR) is defined as the ratio between the investment rate and the rate of output growth.

Problems occur at the same time in many emerging markets on the periphery after a shock in one of them. For example, in the case of the Thai crisis, Japanese banks' exposure to Thailand and their subsequent curtailment of lending to other Asian countries played a key role in the spread of the crisis.

Thailand's GDP growth rates were very high with an average of about 9.0 percent of GDP in between 1987 and 1996. Nevertheless, high economic growth may make an economy more vulnerable to a crisis. But excessively optimistic expectations of persistent high growth can drive both a consumption and an investment boom as well as unsustainably high capital inflows. If there is an external shock, it can suddenly change expectations and cause capital flow reversal and currency crisis.

As for the financial front, to some extent, the rapid development of the financial system during in the late 1980s and early 1990s contributed to Thailand's remarkable growth during the same period. At the same time, inherent weaknesses in the financial sector, itself, in turn, dramatically caused to the country's most severe economic crisis since World War II. The history of commercial banking business in Thailand can be tracked back to 1888 when the British-owned Hong Kong and Shanghai Bank opened a branch in Bangkok to facilitate international trading. Commercial banks are the oldest and largest part of the Thai financial system (see details in table 2.2).

Commercial banks' assets in 1960 stood at 14 percent of GDP. By the end of 2002, total assets of all commercial banks accounted for 127 percent of GDP, equivalent to a compound annual growth rate of 5.5 percent. Bond and equity markets are the second most important part of the Thai financial system. The birth of Thailand's bond market dated back to the 1933 bond issuance by the newly formed Ministry of Finance. The Thai bond market did not grow rapidly until recently because of two main reasons. One is that because of 10 consecutive years of budget surplus between 1987 and 1997, the Thai government did not issue any domestic bonds during that period. The other is that before 1992, the law prohibited limited companies from issuing debenture (Disyatat and Nakornthab, 2003). It should be noted that combined assets of finance companies accounted for nearly one-third of those of commercial banks at the end of 1996. After the 1997 crisis, their number decreased from 91 to 19 with the combined assets accounting for less than one-seventh of those in 1996[11].

[11] The first establishment of finance companies can be tracked back to 1969. Since then, finance companies have frequently been a fragile part of the Thai financial system. The first and second finance companies crises were in 1979 and 1982. The 1997 crisis was the third time (Disyatat and Nakornthab, 2003).

Table 2.3: Major Constituents of Thailand's Financial System (end 2002)

Constituent	First Established	No.	Total assets/values (billion baht)	Share of total financial institution assets (%)
1. Commercial banks				
1.1 Domestic banks	1906	13	5,780	59.4
1.2 Foreign bank branch	1888	18	686	7.0
2. Capital markets				
2.1 SET market capitalisation	1975	n.a.	1,986	n.a.
2.2 Public bonds outstanding	1933	n.a.	1,757	n.a.
2.3 Corporate bonds outstanding	1992	n.a.	543	n.a.
2.4 Securities companies	1953	39	51	0.5
2.5 Mutual fund companies	1975	14	467	4.8
3. Specialised Financial Institutions (SFIs)				
3.1 Government Saving Bank (GSB)	1913	1	600	6.2
3.2 Bank for Agriculture and Agricultural Co-cooperatives (BAAC)	1966	1	396	4.1
3.3 Government Housing Bank (GHB)	1953	1	362	3.7
3.4 IFCT	1959	1	210	2.2
3.5 Export Import Bank (EXIM)	1993	1	48	0.5
3.6 SME Bank (formerly SIFC)	1992	1	13	0.1
3.7 Secondary Mortgage Corp.	1997	1	2	0.02
4. Non-bank financial intermediaries				
4.1 Finance companies	1969	19	254	2.6
4.2 Credit foncier companies	1969	6	6	0.1
4.3 Life insurance companies	1929	26	360	3.7
4.4 Agricultural cooperatives	1916	4,073	67	0.7
4.5 Non agricultural cooperatives	1937	2,333	437	4.5

Source: Disyatat and Nakornthab, 2003

It seems likely that a large number of Thai financial institutions were distressed since the first half of 1997. Troubled financial institutions which concentrated their lending in real estate and property were financed by borrowing from foreign financial institutions. The Financial Institutions Development Fund (FIDF), an organisation linked to the central bank, had lent about US$ 8 billions, 17.5% of which went to Finance One[12], the largest finance company at that time. During the economic slowdown and an increase in interest rate, the task of saving Finance One was very demanding. The company's non-

[12] In terms of assets and liabilities, Finance One held substantial equities in many other finance and securities companies which themselves were vulnerable to the dual pressures of high interest rates and a falling stock market (Corsetti et al., 1998b).

performing loans almost doubled in 1996 and doubled again in the first quarter of 1997. On June 25, 1997, the new finance minister discovered that US$ 28 billions out of US$ 30 billions in international reserves had been committed in forward market interventions for defending the value of the baht and it was the same day that information was leaked that the government would stop assisting Finance One (Corsetti et al., 1998b).

On July 2, 1997, Thailand announced a managed float of the Baht and began to negotiate with the IMF a rescue programme. But the domestic financial crisis was just really at its beginning. Under a plan to revamp the financial sector as part of the general IMF agreement, the central bank suspended 48 finance companies that were already insolvent. Finally, 58 finance companies went bankrupt and were forced to close. It should be noted that some Thai financial institutions were in trouble before the currency crisis. Then the rapid depreciation driven by investors panic significantly increased the burden of their foreign liabilities (Corsetti et al., 1998b).

Clearly, banks in emerging economies are weaker than those of industrialised countries, in terms of capital base, performance and regulations. Nevertheless, it does not necessarily mean that they are ineffective (Bhagwati[13], 2002, Menkhoff and Suwanaporn, 2003). However, before the Asian crisis, Thailand's banks were regarded as a positive element in the economy and Thailand was among the countries classified as resource-efficient (World Bank, 1993). What went wrong in the banking sector in Thailand that made this feature disappear within a few years? In contrast to other literature on the Asian crisis, Menkhoff and Suwanaporn (2003) made an in-depth case study of the lending decisions of Thai commercial banks before the Asian crisis, based on a data set of 560 credit cases which were granted between 1992 and 1996. The study reveals that the structure in lending determinants is significantly consistent to those of industrialised countries. The analysis of ex post default cases shows that ex ante available risk information could have been used better to restrict default.

Did Thailand suffer from bad banking in the sense of deliberately risky loan excesses and moral hazard behaviour? Menkhoff (2000) analysed empirically the performance of Thailand's banks. The study excluded post-crisis period data because the crisis produced a dominant structural break. He pointed out that a sound banking system would have had problems from insolvent borrowers if it faced, as Thailand did, an abrupt currency devaluation of more than 50% (at its peak) associated with a collapsing stock market, a sharp interest rate increase and an economic slowdown. Consequently, the causality between banking and macro problems seems very difficult to disentangle during the post-

[13] It is mentioned that `their banking systems were weaker than those of developed countries, although we can overstate this since Malaysia, for example, had excellent standards and expertise (Bhagwati, 2002, p.57).

crisis period. The finding is that the crisis is not because of the inherent problems of discipline among Thailand's banks but because of rapidly and adversely changing environment that turns former winners into losers.

In fact, the long-term performance of Thailand's financial system is reasonable, compared to other countries' experience. The rapid liberalisation process resulted in severe problems of financial institutions, for example, it increases new kinds of credit risk and market risk. It was also the industrialised countries that were eager to increase their exposure in the crisis region. Thai banks have not operated worse than any other bank in other countries, in terms of efficient allocation and operational efficiency. However, regulatory and macroeconomic policy didn't work properly. As a result, formerly good banking practices became inadequate banking. This result would play an important role for policy implications to be adopted in dealing with the crisis (Menkhoff (2000).

2.3 Crisis Management Policies

2.3.1 The Early Policy Response to the Twin Crises

The background of the Thai economy which includes economic performance in 1995-1996, performance during the crisis year (1997) and performance during the post-crisis period (1998-2000) is summarised in the appendix 2.A.4. The first reaction of monetary authorities to speculative pressures in the foreign exchange market was to avoid a monetary contraction and a significant increase in domestic interest rates. Thailand, like other countries in the region, first sterilised their intervention in the spot and forward markets. Also, Thailand discouraged capital outflows with the introduction of limited capital controls by segmenting the onshore and offshore markets. At the same time, the domestic monetary stance remained untouched. The purpose of a low interest policy in the presence of strong speculative attacks on the currency is concern about the financial conditions. An interest rate increase would worsen the financial conditions, particularly of highly indebted banks, financial institutions and corporations and would further a slowdown in output growth (Corsetti et al., 1998b).

The policy of bailing out financial institutions issued by the government was, actually, a source of money creation. A loose monetary policy aiming to prevent further financial problems and output loss was a very risky strategy. Eventually, it led to a continuous currency depreciation which in turn, increased the burden of foreign-currency liabilities, made the financial sector more vulnerable and increased the cost of bail-out (Corsetti et al., 1998b). In fact, making a choice of switching to tight monetary policy at the right time is a complicated task.

In retrospect, if Thailand had abandoned the fixed exchange rate earlier and allowed the baht to find a level in the market, Thailand could probably have avoided the large loss of reserves and could have had a less painful adjustment. However, this was not so obvious ex ante. The reason to delay abandoning the fixed rate[14] or devalue its level is to avoid inflation, higher interest rates, and increased foreign debt burdens. Thailand also expected that the overvaluation might correct itself if domestic prices fell or the dollar declined in value relative to other currencies (Feldstein, 1999). However, the issue of the appropriate exchange rate regime is still debateable.

2.3.2 The Policy Response under the IMF Programme to the Twin Crises

2.3.2.1 The Debate on the Policy Response to the Crises

The Managing Director of the IMF said that 'in view of the nature of the Asian crisis, the programs[15] had to go far beyond addressing the major fiscal, monetary, or external balance, however, its aim is to strengthen financial systems, improve governance and transparency, restore economic competitiveness, and modernise the legal and regulatory environment'. As for critics of IMF recipes of strict fiscal discipline, the Indonesian case showed an example of sign of flexibility. The first rescue package of October 1997 included very strict fiscal discipline; however, the agreement of June 1999 let Indonesia run the budget deficit below 8.5% of GDP rather than a budget surplus as planned. After that, IMF allowed Korea and Thailand to run a fiscal deficit of 4% of GDP and 2% of GDP respectively. Unfortunately, some observed that these changes came too late (Corsetti et al., 1998b). In addition, the IMF rescue programme was very complex with dozens of detailed conditions and it was difficult to implement the programme under the condition of uncertainty of private lenders about the future health of the crisis economies (Feldstein, 2000).

The appropriate interest rate policy for managing the 1997 financial crisis has been widely debated. The criticism of the IMF high interest policy is that high interest rates were not effective in protecting against currency depreciation and in turn, worsened the crisis by exacerbating banking and corporate

---

[14] A government committing to a fixed exchange rate relative to the US dollar is implicitly committing itself to the same policy of low inflation rate as the United States. If this commitment is believed by domestic firms and workers, they will be likely to keep prices and wages unchanged (Feldstein, 1999, p. 6).

[15] There are two key suggestions which are the conditions under the IMF rescue package: 1) the need to reform the economy, with emphasis on fiscal discipline and financial sector restructuring and 2) the requirement to maintain high interest rates to avoid capital outflows and currency attacks. However, it was criticised that a number of structural elements of the IMF programme were going beyond its traditional macro-adjustment, particularly in the areas of monetary and fiscal tasks. (Corsetti et al (1998b).

bankruptcies and further economic recession (Corsetti et al., 1998b). On the other hand, as mentioned earlier, loose monetary policies at the onset of the twin crisis also exacerbated the currency depreciation and at the same time, deteriorated balance sheets of the banks and firms with high foreign currency denominated liabilities. Nevertheless, with reference to the large recessions in Asian economies after the twin crisis, many seem to agree that the high interest rate policy can have adverse consequences. In summer 1998, interest rates in Thailand significantly fell and stood at the same levels as before the crisis. Thailand faced a credit crunch which did not relate to the level of interest rates. It related to the inability of distressed banks to lend to firms which faced a debt overhang problem (Corsetti et al., 1998b).

The similarities of policy responses to the crises among Asian countries are as follows. Indonesia, Malaysia and Thailand all set up agencies to manage bad assets and all had schemes to inject public money as capital into banks. By contrast, the differences between the policy responses include three main factors: the severity of the problems, political factors, and the structure of the banking system. As to the severity of the problems, Indonesia had a much larger devaluation, stronger depression and greater problems in its banking sector than did Malaysia or Thailand. With reference to political factors, Thailand, Indonesia and Korea had changes of leadership and signed agreements with the IMF that required some policy changes whereas Malaysia maintained its own approach. As for the structure of the banking system, Thailand adopted more of a case-by-case approach to its banks' treatment, whereas Indonesia forced a larger number of banks to adopt more general rules for restructuring (Hawkins, 1999).

2.3.2.2 Policy Response under the IMF Programme in Thailand

During the 1997 financial crisis, Thai economy contracted and banks faced severe liquidity shortages and a sharp deterioration in the quality of their assets. Besides the major fiscal, monetary and external balance policies, the authorities have implemented the various policy measures in order to reform and rehabilitate the financial system (see details in appendix 2.A.5). As mentioned earlier, the aims of financial reform under the IMF programme are to strengthen financial systems, improve governance and transparency, restore economic competitiveness, and modernise the legal and regulatory environment.

Under *the aim of strengthening financial systems*, policy measures (BOT, 2001) include (1) Closure of Finance Companies and Establishment of the Financial Sector Restructuring Authority (FRA) and the Asset Management Corporation (AMC); (2) the Blanket Guarantee of Depositors and Creditors (3) August, 14, 1998 Financial Restructuring Package: This package focused on three main aspects as follows: Intervention, Merger and Privatisation of Weak Institutions; (4) Corporate Debt Restructuring; and (5) Relaxation of Restrictions on Foreign Ownership.

The policy measures with *the aim of improving governance and transparency* include (6) Fit and Proper Criteria for Management; (7) The Establishment of a Credit Bureau; (8) Good Corporate Governance. The Bank of Thailand (BOT) has put forth various measures relating to the practice of good corporate governance, for example, financial institutions are required to disclose information on non-performing loans (NPLs) and lending to related parties and bank's lending to related companies with cross-directorship is restricted.

The policy measures with *the aim of restoring economic competitiveness* include (9) the provision of an Incentive Package for Merger and Acquisition. The authorities allowed the establishment of restricted-licensed bank through merger or acquisition of at least five entities of finance companies, finance and securities companies and credit foncier companies with good track records and stable financial standing.

The policy measures under *the aim of modernising the legal and regulatory environment* include (10) the Supervision Standards Upgrade. It includes guidelines on accruing interest income, asset valuation, loan review, asset classification and provisioning.

2.4 Consequences for the Banking Sector after the Crisis: Successes and Remaining Policy Issues

During 1997-2002, Thailand undertook numerous policy measures as mentioned in section 2.3 to restore stability in the financial system. Since 2001, financial institutions have returned to profitability, as a result of improvements in business operations, risk management and, importantly, their capital bases (BOT, 2003). This section discusses what happened to the banking sector after Thailand imposed all the related measures under the crisis management policies. The remaining policy issues related to those areas are also addressed.

2.4.1 Banks' Balance Sheets Development

The size of Thailand's banking sector relative to GDP is large. Based on the study by Disyatat and Nakornthab (2003), as shown in figure 2.1: the ratio of commercial banks' claims on private sector to GDP of 22 countries averaged during 1997-2002, Thailand's ratio was as high as 97 percent, compared with the sample average of 83 percent. It can be seen from the study on the assessment of the country's financial structure[16] that in spite of significant declines in bank loans following the 1997 financial crisis, Thailand greatly relied on bank-finance, compared to other Asian countries. Interestingly, while Hong Kong and Singapore have larger banking sectors than Thailand, their

[16] The assessment of the country's financial structure can be found by the relative proportions of the value of bank loans to the private sector, stock market capitalisation and corporate bonds outstanding to those added up (Disyatat and Nakornthab, 2003).

financial structures are more balanced (see figure 2.2), partly due to their deeper stock markets (Disyatat and Nakornthab 2003). Regarding deposit mobilisation, a shift from bank deposits to non-bank financial institutions[17] has been observed in the global financial markets and also in Thailand. In fact, between 1997 and

Figure 2.1: Private sector liabilities in percent of GDP (1997-2002 average)

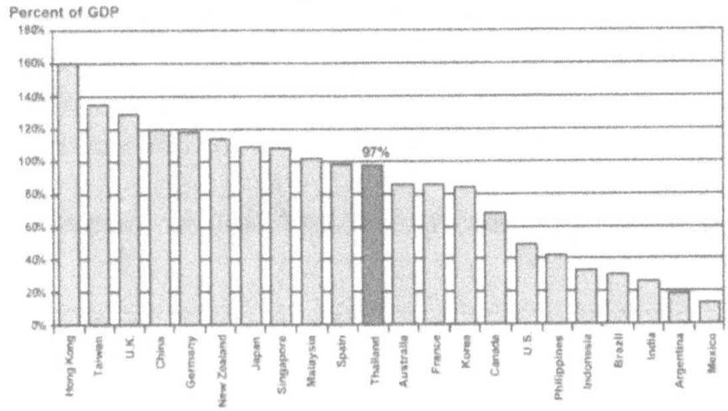

Source: Disyatat and Nakornthab (2003)

Figure 2.2: Composition of Private Sector Financing at 2001

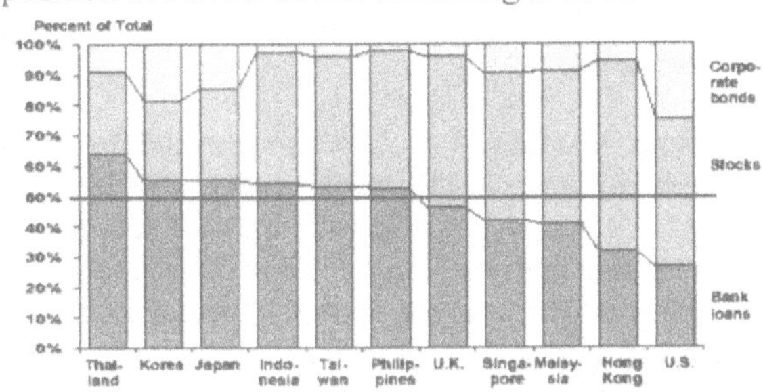

Source: Disyatat and Nakornthab (2003)

2002, growth in household deposits in non-bank financial institutions increased by more than five times. However, the size of savings held with non-bank financial institutions in Thailand remains low, compared to the size of commercial bank deposits (Disyatat and Nakornthab, 2003).

The Thai financial sector has gradually rebounded since the crisis of 1997. The improvements in banks' balance sheets have been reflected in the decline in the level of non-performing loans (NPLs) from their peak in 1999. In fact, NPLs

---

[17] Non-bank financial institutions include life insurances, pension funds and mutual funds (Disyatat and Nakornthab (2003). It should be noted that unlike households in developed countries, Thai households tend to prefer investment in real estate to investment in financial assets, except for bank deposits. In fact, when the economy picked up sharply in early 2002, the value of house and land significantly increased (Senivongs na Ayudhya et al., 2003).

in the Thai financial system have steadily declined from their peak of 45.0 percent of total credit outstanding in the financial system in 1998 to about 15.6 percent[18] at end-2002 (BOT, 2003). The capitalisation has significantly improved. At the end of Q1-2003, the ratio of existing loan loss reserves to required reserves stood at 138 percent and the BIS ratios of capital to risk assets of locally incorporated banks stood at 12.5 percent, 4 percent higher than the level required by the Bank of Thailand. Recently, balance sheets of the banking sector have rebounded to profitability. Pre-provision profits have gradually turned positive since 2000 (Disyatat and Nakornthab, 2003). Nevertheless, the large overhang of NPLs has been challenging for the economic recovery.

Table 2.4: Corporate Performance in 2001-2002, Dupont Analysis of Listed Companies on SET

	1997	1998	1999	20002001		2002
D/E	4.9	3.5	4.0	4.5	3.4	2.3
Asset to Debt Ratio	1.2	1.3	1.2	1.2	1.3	1.4
Asset Turnover (%)	44	44	48	56	62	73
Profit Margin (%)	-44	7	-9	-6	5	8
ROA (%)	-19	3	-4	-3	3	6
ROE (%)	-115	15	-22	-17	14	20

Source: Bank of Thailand, 2003, p. 11

Senivongs na Ayudhya et al., (2003) identified the interrelations between the balance sheets of households, corporations, and banks. Weakness in the balance sheets of one sector can affect the balance sheets of other sectors. The study demonstrates that both the corporate and household sectors have gradually improved their balance sheets since the 1997 financial crisis. Based on Dupont-type ratios, namely the operating assets turnover ratio, the ratio of adjusted EBIT /sales ratio and the return on assets[19], they show obvious improvements as the country returned to economic growth since 2001 (see table 2.4). However, a solvency weakness has been observed in the corporate sector. Importantly, the average cost of borrowing which continued to further exceed MLR (Minimum Lending Rates) suggested that firms had not benefited from lower interest rates since debt was rescheduled rather than really restructured. Even if firms are able to restructure their debt, they cannot be sure that banks will be willing to extend

[18] The figure is calculated according to the new Bank of Thailand's definition of NPLs which has been recently revised to reflect international standards. Thus, the current definition of NPLs includes the entire amount of loans which are classified as substandard, doubtful, doubtful of loss and loss (Bank of Thailand, 2003).

[19] The ratio of turnover to operating assets is defined as Sales/ Average Operating Assets; the ratio of adjusted EBIT over sales is defined as Earnings Before Interest and Taxes (EBIT) – Other Income/Sales and the Return on Assets (ROA) = Net Income/Average Total Assets (Senivongs na Ayudhya et al., 2003).

new credit to them unless they show the banks significant changes in their management and corporate governance in line with prudent business and financial management (Senivongs na Ayudhya et al., 2003).

Based on a comparison of cross-sections in 1997 and 2000 of balance sheet data of 100 firms randomly selected from listed firms on the Stock Exchange of Thailand (SET), accounting for about 25 per cent in terms of number or about 40 per cent in terms of market capitalisation of non-financial firms, one study finds that larger firms in Thailand have been moving to capital markets in order to diversify their sources of funding because of more stringent bank lending conditions and their efforts to reduce debt loads (Molnar, 2003). As a result, the share of bank borrowing among sources of debt financing of manufacturing firms has declined. The development of the corporate bond market was facilitated by the establishment of pricing benchmarks. Besides increasing bond issues, manufacturing firms have relied more on trade credits compared to the situations before 1997.

2.4.2 The Credit Channel of Monetary Transmission[20] after the Crisis

After the crisis, the monetary authorities progressively eased the stance of monetary policy. Short-term interest rates declined from about 20 percent in 1998 to about 1.5 percent by mid-2001. Nevertheless, bank-lending rates adjusted slowly and private credit grew slowly (IMF, 2002). Is the monetary policy transmission mechanism working? An IMF (2002) study indicates that there is weak transmission from the policy rate (1.7 percent) to bank-lending. At the same time, shocks to bank-lending have weak effects on output.[21] In sum, supply side effects in private credit do not seem to work efficiently. By contrast,

[20] The Channels of monetary policy transmission include four main channels—*interest rate channel, exchange rate channel, credit channel and asset price channel*. The interest rate channel is the standard Keynesian channel of monetary transmission. For example, contractionary monetary policy raises short term nominal interest rates. According to the exchange rate channel, an increase in domestic interest rates attracts foreign capital which appreciates the real exchange rate and leads to a fall in net exports. The credit channel includes the bank-lending channel and the balance sheet channel. Fundamentally, banks play an important role in financial markets by maintaining close relationships with borrowers and overcoming problems of information asymmetries in credit markets. A monetary contraction which decreases bank reserves causes banks to reduce the supply of their loans. This leads to a fall in investment if firms do not have access to other sources of borrowing. The balance sheet channel refers to the weakening of corporate balance sheets when interest rates rise and free cash flows fall. The asset price channel focuses on the behaviour of equity and other asset prices. A monetary contraction normally comes with a decrease in equity prices since investors move their investment from stocks to bonds (IMF, 2002).

[21] In order to show the significance of bank-lending in the transmission process, a comparison is made between the impulse responses with and without the bank-lending channel operating. A large difference in the impulse response would indicate that bank-lending is an important channel (IMF, 2002, p. 11).

interest rate increases seem to directly affect firms' investment decisions as the market value of firms drop or corporate balance sheets weaken. Interestingly, asset prices seem to transmit monetary shocks.

Until the summer of 1998, although the price of credit in Asia had significantly fallen, compared to the peaks during the crisis, banks which experienced financial distress were unwilling to lend to corporations which suffered from debt overhang and had hardly any access to working capital and trade credits (Corsetti et al., 2001a). In Thailand, a comprehensive approach to corporate debt restructuring [22] was established and modelled on the 'London Approach' which was used for out-of-court debt workouts. It is voluntary, case-by-case and market based and it is associated with an active role of the government as facilitator or independent intermediary.

As for the corporate performance, debt levels have fallen from their post-crisis peak and returns and corporate cash flows have gradually stabilised (IMF, 2002) (see also table 2.4). At the same time, firms still face the difficulty of accessing bank loans. This is confirmed by a recent study suggesting that firms were not able to switch effectively from foreign borrowing to domestic borrowing (Senivongs na Ayudhya et al., 2003, p.5). This was because domestic banks were reluctant to lend to the firms owing to uncertainties of the prospects of economic recovery and debt restructuring and bankruptcy. As a result, solving current financial problems of high level of NPLs on bank balance sheets will contribute to the importance of the bank-lending channel.

2.4.3 Bank Disintermediation

The financial structure of Thailand has changed since the 1997 crisis, in particular, the decline in bank credit. With respect to commercial banks' sources of funds, from the data comparison between 1994-96 and 2000-02, the share of deposits, which had fallen substantially during the 1997/1998 crisis, increased again following the subsequent economic recovery and even surpassed its pre-crisis level by 2002. On the other hand, the share of foreign liabilities with a lengthening profile of maturity substantially declined. This evidence indicates that liquidity risk is not a major concern for Thai banks today.

As for the use of funds, private credit in commercial banks' asset portfolios notably dropped. By contrast, investments in foreign assets and government securities increased (Disyatat and Nakornthab, 2003). The causes of these developments were empirically studied in a recent study by the OECD (Molnar, 2003). The study is based on micro-data on all 13 domestic commercial banks and 13 foreign bank branches, accounting for above 95

[22] The corporate debt workout process in Thailand includes an informal workout process which has been newly created and a formal workout process in the court which has been amended (Bank of Thailand, 2003).

percent of the market in terms of loans or assets, between the third quarter of 2000 and fourth quarter of 2001. The study reveals that the decline in bank lending is prominently attributed to more strict regulations concerning capital adequacy associated with the effect from the 1997 financial crisis, both in the form of NPLs and foreclosed assets in bank's balance sheets. Interestingly, domestic commercial banks in Thailand have been more affected by these factors than foreign bank branches (Molnar, 2003, p. 6). In response to the drop in lending growth and a decline in profits after the crisis, banks have been restructuring their strategies by diversifying their customer base[23] and scope of activities.

The banks' balance sheets have been improved; nevertheless, the large overhang of NPLs still has not been removed. While direct state intervention in the financial sector was considerable, the strategy for corporate debt restructuring focused on facilitating private party resolution. At the peak, the Corporate Debt Restructuring Advisory Committee (CDRAC)[24] was advising on deals worth almost 50 percent of GDP. More recently, the Thai Asset Management Corporation (TAMC) was established and has taken care of most of the NPLs from the state-owed banks (IMF, 2002). Despite progress on corporate debt restructuring, corporate debt levels remain still high. Debt restructuring strategies[25] have concentrated more on debt rescheduling than debt reduction. The reason for this is that in principle, creditors try to prolong the process of loss recognition and preserve the capital. Normally, creditors want to have as little reduction in the net present value (NPV) of their debt as possible. Hence, distressed assets of both the corporate sector and its financial sector counterpart remain high. However, it should be kept in mind that the fundamentally microeconomic restructuring process has its way and takes time (IMF, 2002). Until then, the financial sector cannot fully play its role as financial intermediary in facilitating sustained economic growth.

[23] Among of the fastest growing customer segments of the banks are individuals and small and medium-size enterprises. As for the scope of their activities, banks expanded their activities and the border line between banking and securities business disappeared (Molnar, 2003).

[24] The voluntary Corporate Debt Restructuring Advisory Committee (CDRAC) process (now winding down) was established in 1998 and was set up to help bring debtors and creditors to the negotiating table (IMF, 2002). Between 1998 and end January 2003, CDRAC successfully restructured 10,322 cases with the total value of 1,382.9 billion Baht, whereas 1,683 additional cases with a total value of 420.3 billion Baht were sent to the courts for adjudication (Bank of Thailand, 2003).

[25] From the author's experience in private corporate debt workout in Thailand, debt restructuring strategies can be classified into four main groups as follows: debt rescheduling, debt conversion (debt for equity swaps), debt write-off and others, for example debt-buy back.

2.4.4 An Increase in Foreign Bank Participation

Feldstein (2002) pointed out that countries with strong banking systems and good bank supervision like Singapore prevented the difficulties that occurred in the crisis countries. Corsetti et al., (2001a) also gave similar comments. In the case of East Asia, most foreign banks lend to local banks and local banks lend to domestic corporations. If a foreign bank operated locally, it would be more concerned with the stability of domestic corporations and would be unlikely to call in loans immediately and repatriate funds since this would harm the foreign bank directly. The presence of foreign banks could mitigate some of the problems that occur with weak domestic supervision and regulation. Besides the positive effects of foreign bank ownership, one of the objections to this is a matter of sovereignty because traditionally, banks have been used for political reasons through direct lending (Corsetti et al., 2001a).

In addition, foreign banks can contribute to the stability of the domestic deposit base. A widespread episode called 'flight to quality' during the Thai financial crisis was observable. Depositors in Thailand shifted funds from finance companies and small banks toward larger banks, particularly foreign financial institutions. Their market share of deposits in Thailand increased from 2 percent of total deposits at the end of 1996 to 5 percent at the end of 1997 (Agenor, 2001).

As for the ownership structure, before the 1997 financial crisis, all locally-incorporated banks in Thailand were majority owned by Thai citizens. After the crisis, most banks needed large amounts of new capital which they could not raise from local investors who were also affected by the crisis. As a result, at end-2000, 4 out of 13 locally-incorporated banks turned to be majority-owned by foreigners. Their equity accounted for 16.4 percent of total locally-incorporated banks' equity (BOT, 2001). It should be noted that foreign banks are now allowed to take a majority stake in domestic banks in Thailand; however, it can only be held for ten years. This seems to discourage foreign banks from buying. In contrast, Malaysia still limits foreign ownership of banks at only 30 percent of total stake (Hawkins, 1999).

2.5 Lessons from the Thai Financial Crisis

The 1997 financial crisis was the worst in the Thailand's history. It ended a period of unprecedented economic growth. Since then, Thailand has been working to build a sustainable economy based upon a safe and sound financial sector (BOT, 2001). However, in order to ensure that financial institutions are ready to face the dynamism of global forces of change, there are still major challenges ahead. This section draws some lessons from the crisis management policies for the banking sector in Thailand after the crisis period, and from financial crises more generally[26]. The framework of this section is close to the work of Kawai et al., (2001)[27].

2.5.1 Crisis Management Strategies

Thailand is not the first country to experience a financial sector crisis after financial sector liberalisation. Examples of this are the U.S. in the mid-1980s, Sweden, Finland and Norway in the late 1980s and early 1990s and Mexico in 1994-95. Financial history holds some lessons on how to manage crises. However, managing financial crises is still one of the most difficult tasks to confront policymakers, in particular when it includes banking problems. The policymakers must quickly decide to issue policy measures, sometimes in eye of a crisis with imperfect information (BIS, 1999).

Kawai et al. (2001, p. 33-40) presents three interesting policy lessons that should be heeded in managing crises and contagion. One is that countries should mobilise timely external liquidity of sufficient magnitude associated with sound policies to restore market confidence. Second is that bailing in private foreign creditors at times of crisis is essential. Third is that there is no one prescription for monetary and fiscal policy that fits in all crises episodes. Bäckström (1997) states that during the Swedish banking crisis in the early 1990s, the authorities chose the method to disclose expected loan losses and assign realistic values to real estates and other assets. The level of valuation was realistic; however, great pains were taken to give a transparent picture of how the crisis was being managed in order to revive the confidence of Sweden's creditors.

As for the 1994 Mexican financial crisis, the IMF and the U.S. government took exceptional steps to provide a $50 billion rescue package to allow the Mexican government to maintain debt service. This was criticised for allegedly encouraging moral harzard on the part of investors (Eichengreen and Portes, 1997). It is mentioned that the results of the Nordic and Asian crisis management have been quite good (Ingves, 2003). As for the case of Thailand, the following are main lessons that we can draw from its experience.

2.5.1.1 The Closure of Nonviable Financial Companies

Thailand experienced a financial crisis in 1983-87 that was associated with a slowdown in the economy, globally high interest rates, and fraud and mismanagement on the part of several finance companies and banks. The crisis started at the finance companies which were poorly supervised and had engaged in heavy speculations in shares and real estate. A total of 24 finance companies

---

[26] See for example, Alba et al., 1999, Bäckström, 1997, Caprio and Vittas, 1995, Eichengreen and Portes, 1997, Kawai et al., 2001, Krugman, 1999, Mishkin, 2000 and Stone, 2002.

[27] They emphasise four groups of nine lessons as follows; preventing crises and contagion, managing crises and contagion, resolving the systemic consequences of crises, and strengthening regional arrangements to complement the global financial architecture to help in prevention, management, and resolution (Kawai et al., 2000, p. 24-47.

was subsequently closed, and nine others merged into two new companies. Consequently, despite the lack of an explicit deposit insurance scheme, the resolution of the mid-80s crisis reinforced the belief that depositors and banks would be bailed out if financial institutions were insolvent (see Alba et al., 1999).

The 1997 financial crisis seems to be more severe than the one in 1983-87 because the problems occurred not only in financial companies but also in many commercial banks. It was estimated that at the peak the non-performing loans (NPLs) stood at almost 50 percent of loans in Thailand. On June 27, 1997, the operations of 16 insolvent and liquidity-strapped finance companies were suspended and later on August 5, 1997, an additional 42 finance companies became insolvent and were suspended (see BOT, 2001). This experience suggests that these unclear procedures of resolution of nonviable financial companies exacerbated the public panic. It is accepted that the first task of financial restructuring is to separate out the viable from the nonviable financial institutions to the extent possible (Stone, 2002). To stop the crisis, the government announced on August 5, 1997 a blanket guarantee, in local currency terms, for both depositors and creditors of domestic and foreign financial institutions operating in Thailand (BOT, 2001).

Kawai (et al., 2001) also agree that the experience in East Asia has shown that domestic procedures of banking sector resolutions were frequently inadequate. One lesson we learned from the case of Thailand is that procedures of diagnostic reviews of bank portfolios, which were not fully based on internationally accepted classification rules and accounting principles, identification of viable and nonviable financial institutions and closure nonviable financial institutions were probably inadequate. In contrast, the related procedures of dealing with resolution of nonviable financial institutions, like liquidation, temporary nationalisation, merger and acquisition, etc. were reasonable.

The authority attempted to resolve the problems using a least-cost approach. A capital write-down would first be ordered, thus forcing the existing shareholders to shoulder a loss prior to the injection of new capital by the Financial Institutions Development Fund (FIDF). Other lessons learned from the first three years after the crisis (1997-1999) indicate that keeping intervened banks open would provide continuation of services to the customers and prevent deterioration of assets. However, keeping them as state banks would not be practical because of a lack of management expertise. As a result, Thai and foreign strategic investors have been invited to invest in the banks as their expertise would be needed to revive the banks' operation (BOT, 2001).

2.5.1.2 Bank and Corporate Debt Restructuring

Positively thinking, the first lesson we can draw from the financial crisis is that it has brought forces of change to Thailand's financial sector. Because Thailand is a small, market-oriented and open economy with linkages to the international financial markets, it is very important for domestic financial institutions to be alert to the global changes and learn the lessons in their competitive strategies to create value added (BOT, 2003). Since 1997, the authorities have initiated many reform measures to correct the existing weaknesses and strengthen the supervisory framework based in a market-oriented manner. One example is the introduction of a minimum capital requirement ratio at 8.5 percent, slightly above the Bank for International Settlements' (BIS) standard. The main area of the supervisory reform is the compliance with the BIS 25 Core Principles of Effective Banking Supervision and the New Basel Capital Accord. This reform is still in the process of preparation (see BOT, 2003).

The second lesson we can draw is that the authorities lacked adequate knowledge in dealing with the sale of bad assets. The evidence is that often the highest bids received were about 25-30 percent of book value which was below what the authorities regarded as the minimum acceptable. In those cases, some packages of loans were offered on a profit-sharing basis in a later auction. The advantage of profit sharing arrangements is that they enable the authorities to share in any increases in asset value that may occur later on as the economy recovers. The disadvantage is that the Financial Sector Restructuring Agency (FRA) cannot estimate beforehand how much revenue will eventually occur and be available.

With reference to the blanket guarantee by the government, it stopped the panic, on the other hand, it caused a huge future burden, accounting for 44 percent of GDP as of 2001[28] (IMF, 2002). In this regard, the third lesson arising from Thailand's experience is that the IMF's assistance must include a condition on the government's willingness to operate a bank restructuring programme that limits moral hazard. The large depositors and bank shareholders must share the costs of restructuring and recapitalising insolvent institutions (Eichengreen and Portes, 1997, p. 218).

Regarding the corporate restructuring on a large scale, Stone (2002) pointed out that successful completion of restructuring requires a government to take the lead in establishing restructuring priorities, addressing market failures, reforming the legal and tax systems and importantly, dealing with obstacles

---

[28] As for the gross cost of financial sector restructuring (accounting for 44 percent of GDP as of 2001), about one-third of it has been financed through the issuance of governance bonds. The residual gross costs (31 percent of GDP) are funded by the FIDF, either explicitly on its balance sheet (12 percent of GDP), or implicitly in the form of off-balance sheet (contingent) liabilities (19 percent of GDP) (IMF, 2002).

caused by powerful interest groups. This has been the case in Thailand where a government in strong collaboration with the private sector (The Foreign Banks' Associations, Thai Commercial Banks Associations, Financial companies Associations, Thai Chambers Associations and The Federation of Thai Industries) has played an active role in this matter.

In addition, the experience of the past years shows that there has been a reshaping of bank-firm relationships in the five year period (1997-2001). Banks in Thailand have diversified their portfolio into securities investment and off-balance sheet activities. Bank lending has decreased because of the large overhang of NPLs. At the same time, firms have managed to acquire funds for investment by relying less on bank loans and moving more toward bond financing. The fourth lesson that we can draw from this reshaping is that diversification of banking portfolios and firms' capital structure seems to develop in a good direction. However, the NPL problem should also continuously be monitored by both banks and firms (Molnar, 2003).

2.5.2 Crisis Prevention Strategies

There is a conventional saying 'Kunwei-deekua-kae' in Thailand which means 'an ounce of prevention is worth a pound of cure'. This captures well one of the lessons to be drawn from the Thai crisis (Eichengreen and Portes, 1997). A positive side effect to come from a crisis such as the one experienced in Thailand is that misguided practices and policy weaknesses become very readily apparent to everyone. This led the authorities to initiate an ambitious program of financial sector reform to prevent a similar crisis from occurring again. The main crisis prevention strategies that we can draw from the recent crisis are as follows:

2.5.2.1 Creating Early Warning Systems

As mentioned earlier in Kaminsky and Reinhart (1998 and 1999), both currency and banking crises are preceded by weak and deteriorating economic fundamentals. Based on data of 102 financial crises in 20 countries, Kaminsky's study (1998) concludes that the Asian crises are not a new phenomenon. The 1997 Asian crises, as well as previous crises in other regions, occur when the economic conditions are in distress. As a result, policy makers need to identify weaknesses and imbalances early enough before the crises occur. Interestingly, Babson and Kamin[29] (1999) developed a modified 'early warning system (EWS)' approach to identify the roles of domestic and external factors in Latin America's crises. The finding is that when the effects of adverse external shocks are removed from the simulated probabilities of devaluation in Latin America,

---

[29] They constructed models to simulate the probability of crises over the 1981-1998 periods. Then they re-simulated the models in order to identify the separate contributions to the probabilities of crisis from domestic, external-balance, and external-shock variables.

the resultant simulated devaluation probabilities are still high. This indicates that devaluation crises in Latin America primarily are a function of domestic policy and economic imbalances, and exogenous external factors play as a secondary role.

Early warning systems are suggested as one of the instruments for avoiding future crises. Beckmann and Menkhoff (2003) reviewed recent academic work on Early Warning Systems (EWSs) and assessed the application of new methods in extracting information from fundamentals. They conclude that creating effective EWSs is a difficult task, particularly the forecast of exchange rates, and that different approaches of EWSs give different results. They also point out clearly that some core economic indicators seem to change before the occurrence of the financial crises. The complexity of changes is considerable; as a result, one should not solely rely on a single indicator or on a small set of indicators as early warning systems. Edison (2000) shared the similar comments and further suggested that the models are useful as a diagnostic tool; however, they must be complemented by more standard country surveillance and cannot substitute for such surveillance.

How can the theoretical views be applied in practice? The international financial organisations, like IMF and World Bank, and the international community at large are in the process of designing and implementing EWSs under the Financial Sector Assessment Program (FSAP). FSAP is widely recognised by participating countries and by the international community as an important instrument for diagnosis and analysis of potential vulnerabilities in the financial sectors of member countries (IMF and World Bank, 2003). The FSAP was initiated in May 1999 as a voluntary programme in response to calls by international communities to facilitate early detection of financial sector vulnerabilities and enhance effective collaboration between the World Bank and the IMF. The complementary analytical tools and assessments under FSAP include three main elements[30] ranging form the systematic analysis of Financial Soundness Indicators (FSIs) and stress testing[31] used to identify risks and vulnerabilities to the assessment of the broader financial stability policy

---

[30] The FSAP includes three main elements: (1) the systematic analysis of Financial Soundness Indicators (FSIs) and stress testing used to indentify risks and vulnerabilities; (2) the assessment of standards and codes used to assess institutional and regulatory structures; and (3) the assessment of the broader financial stability policy framework which consists of systemic liquidity arrangements, governance and transparency framework, and financial safety nets and insolvency regimes (IMF and World Bank, 2003).

[31] The main areas of risks under the FSAP stress testing experience of 28 countries, including six industrial countries, include interest rate risk, exchange rate risk, credit risk, liquidity risk, equity and/or real estate price risk, commodity price risk and other types of risks (IMF and WB, 2003).

framework. The Bank of Thailand is one of the central banks and supervisory agencies cooperating in the FSAP.

2.5.2.2 Reducing Vulnerability

Getting Macroeconomic Policies Right and Sound Banking

To reduce the risk in the future, the experience of the past decade suggests that the emerging market economies should focus on the following three matters: 1) avoid large current account deficits which occur from mismanagement of real exchange rates; 2) avoid international balance sheet mismatches and also avoid to have large proportions of short-term foreign currency debt; and 3) improve the domestic banking system and banking regulation in order to reduce the risk of a credit boom, poor credit risks, and inappropriate foreign exposure (see Feldstein, 2000, Mishkin, 2000 and Kawai et al., 2001). One way to strengthen the local banking system is to enhance foreign bank participation in the domestic banking system as mentioned earlier (Feldstein, 2000 and Corsetti et al., 2001). However, the proportion of private and public sector debt in total debt does not matter because in crisis situations the difference between the two categories blurs (Pesenti and Tille, 2000). Mishkin (2000) also added other financial policies to prevent financial crises which include for example a reduction of the role of state-owned financial institutions and a development of legal and judicial systems which are consistent with the international standards.

Increasing International Liquidity

Feldstein's (1999) proposal of self-protection for emerging market economies that want to avoid the distressing effects of 1997 crisis is *an increase in international liquidity*. Krugman (1999, p. 470) shared a similar proposal of the provision of emergency credit lines which not only provide lender-of-last resort facilities to banks or provide balance of payments financing but also make up the credit being lost by firms so as to allow firms to continue their operation. It includes three facilities. One is an avoidance of excessive short-term debt. Second is an accumulation foreign exchange reserves[32]. For example, China's reserves accounted for $US 140 billion which gives a strong signal to international investors that China will hardly devalue the yuan. Third is the creation of a collaterized credit facility[33]. In the recent 1997 crisis, the American banks alone had outstanding loans and investment of more than $5,000 billion in

---

[32] A country could substantially lower the net cost of holding reserves by investing its reserves in a broader range of assets, for example, US treasury bills or liquid assets with higher yields like US corporate stock (Feldstein, 1999, p. 15-16).

[33] It was mentioned that the IMF should not have sent the message that the Asian crisis countries were corrupt and incompetent and needed fundamental change. Why would creditors still want to roll over their loans to Korea when they had been warned by the IMF? Not mentioning that the problem in the crisis countries was one of temporary illiquidity rather than permanent insolvency worsened the situations. By contrast, the IMF sent that message in the currency crises of the 1980s (Feldstein, 2000).

emerging markets whereas the IMF had less than $200 billion of total lending capacity of which $42 billion went to Brazil alone for a 1998 package. Consequently, to access private credit lines from banks and other investors in industrial countries is more challenging. One way to continue getting the private credit lines for additional foreign reserves is to create a collaterized credit facility[34]. This way of self-protection can solve the financial problem caused by temporary international illiquidity.

Shifting toward Risk-based Incentives to Supplement Regulations

McDonough (2003) highlighted the interesting point that a flexible, market-based and case-by-case approach should be applied to deal with complex and changing financial crises. He elaborated that it is generally agreed that in order to achieve sustained and stable growth, both capital-exporting and capital-importing countries should have a sound and stable macroeconomic environment and well-functioning and robust financial systems which are supported by a dynamic and adaptive policy regime[35]. With reference to changing and complex linkages between domestic and international markets through internationalisation of local banking, equity, debt, and currency markets and the funding structures, the resolution of financial crises can be neither a single piece of financial engineering nor an agreement between the official lenders and private creditors. It is a process of incorporating a number of elements among them.

Thailand has undertaken various policy measures to restore financial stability. The authorities made efforts to tackle the fundamental structural weaknesses of financial institutions. The crisis prevention policies (see also BOT, 2003) are 1) reconstructing the architecture of the financial system (Financial Sector Master Plan), 2) drafting the Financial Institutions Business Act, which combines the financial institutions acts for commercial banks, finance companies, and credit foncier into one act. The act will empower the central bank to oversee and supervise financial institutions based on consolidated supervision. 3) improving risk based management techniques (BIS standard according to the New Basel Capital Accord and 4) establishing a credit bureau to prevent bad assets and the issuance of limited deposit insurance.

Importantly, the authorities encourage a market-oriented risk-based regulatory reform which provides more room for financial institutions to adapt

---

[34] The forms of a collaterized credit facility can be as follows: one would be trade receivables, i.e., the export earnings in hard curencies of the domestic firms, the second would be a voluntary arrangement between an emerging market government and a group of foreign banks and other financial institutions (see more details in Feldstein, 1999).

[35] The dynamic and adaptive regime is the country that realises the following long list: strong financial system, sustained fiscal account, low inflation, credible and coherent monetary and exchange rate policies, moderate external and internal indebtedness, sustained current account, and adequate domestic saving rates (McDonough, 2003).

their business models to match their strategy and target niche. It is believed that this reform will help financial institutions to cope with the evolving business and their risk profiles and that the reform increases the responsibility and accountability of the management groups of financial institutions (BOT, 2003). It should be noted that developing effective supervision in order to ensure meaningful and effective compliance with prudential rules is difficult and time-consuming but essential (Caprio and Vittas, 1995). However, national authorities should also anticipate the need for reforms and carry them on in times of relative financial calm (Dziobek and Pazarbasioglu, 1998).

2.5.2.3 The Role of Institutions: The New Asian Challenge

It is generally agreed among the East Asian Economic Group, ASEAN[36] plus 3 (China, Japan and Korea) to establish a new Asian economic institution with an aim to deepen economic cooperation within the region and to coordinate its economic relations with the rest of the world. One of the resolutions arising after the Asian twin crisis for the new Millennium is `never again′. The resolution aims to complete internal reforms in order to obviate future crises and any need to call in outside resources (Bergsten, 2000). Kawai et al., (2001) also proposed a similar idea of regional financial coordination which may include a regional consultation and economic surveillance and a regional financing facility which can help to close the gap if there are long delays to receive globally available resources.

The East Asian economy accounted for about one third of the world economy and more than half of the world's monetary reserves. However, this region was excessively dependent on the international financial institutions based on `Washington consensus′ from the authorities of the United States and the private market, predominantly Anglo-Saxon. Consequently, East Asian economies seem in need to find their own way of solving their financial crises (Bergsten, 2000).

Bergsten (2000) also justified that one of the important implications of regional institutionalisation in East Asia is that an effective East Asian grouping would produce fundamental changes in the systemic configuration. For example, China and Malaysia tended to support capital control mechanisms with the combination of aggressive monitoring and regulating the activities of hedge funds to prevent the future financial crises, on the contrary, Hong Kong concentrated in market-oriented mechanisms. The creation of new Asian economic institutions is already underway and when it is ready, it could bring numerous positive results in terms of financial stability and economic progress for the world as a whole as well as Asia itself (Bergsten, 2000).

---

[36] The Association of Southeast Asian Nations (ASEAN) includes original members, which are Brunei, Indonesia, Malaysia, the Philippines, Singapore, Thailand and four recent additions (Cambodia, Laos PDR, Myanmar, and Vietnam).

2.5.3 Others: Implications for Creditors

As an international organisation with the aim to promote international financial stability, the IMF could play an important role in reducing the risk of future crises in three ways: firstly, initiate to bring borrowers and lenders together to solve the crisis; secondly, provide accurate assessments of the debtor countries' solvency including information on monetary and fiscal conditions; and thirdly, provide early warnings of balance sheet mismatches to central banks in the creditor countries like the United States of America, Europe and Japan (Feldstein, 2002). Recently, creditors and international organisations have developed new procedures for resolving debt crises. Many crises in the 1990s, for example in Thailand, Korea and Indonesia very much related to credits and loans extended to banks and corporations (private sector). As a result, the development of new mechanisms for crisis resolution, Collective Action Clauses (CACs)[37] in international bonds, is on the way (see more in Eichengreen et al., 2003).

With reference to the role of Japan, the leading regional economy, there are two main aspects. One is that the economic weakness in Japan with a long period of economic recession since early 1990s contributed to the Asian crisis through a reduced demand for imports from the Asian region. The other is that when banks and firms in Asian countries that had borrowed heavily from Japan were affected by the currency shocks, the financial outlook of Japanese banks already weakened by a stagnant domestic economy correspondingly deteriorated. In contrast, the role of the U.S. in the Mexican crisis of 1994-95 was in a strong cyclical upswing (Corsetti et al., 1998b).

2.6 Concluding Remarks

Currency and banking crises are not a new episode. Crises seem to act like a hydra: whenever something is learned from experience, new characteristics of a subsequent crisis emerge (Beckmann and Menkhoff, 2003). Crises can be regarded as dramatic episodes of volatility; they were intensified by financial globalisation over the past decade and by the large players in speculative attacks. Lessons from history provide knowledge about crises. In short, currency crises occur when internal economic conditions are incompatible with the external conditions set for the currency. In the post-World War II period, the Bretton Woods systems were exposed to currency crises. Countries confronted

---

[37] Collective Action Clauses specify procedures for selecting a bondholders' representative and enumerate his responsibilities, include majority enforcement clauses in which the litigation decision must be made by a requisite fraction of the bondholders (for example 25 percent) and require that all funds thereby recovered be distributed in proportion to the principal amount. They specify the share of the bondholders whose vote is sufficient for amending payment terms like the timing and amount of principal and interest (Eichengreen et al., 2003, p. 3).

currency crises if competitive trends had changed the equilibrium real exchange rate which would require an adjustment of the nominal parity. Nevertheless, in practice, countries were reluctant to voluntarily change their parities because they might face massive capital outflows.

International economic crises will probably continue to occur in the future as they have for centuries. Crises tended to be more country-specific in the past, whereas today crises tend to occur in several emerging markets at the same time. Emerging market countries that want to avoid the devasting effects of such crises must protect themselves.

Emerging market countries should avoid external and internal imbalance through a judicious combination of monetary, exchange rate and fiscal policies. Importantly, they should strengthen the domestic banking system and banking regulation on a par with international standards and best practice which are based on risk-based supervision. In addition, higher standards on corporate governance i.e. mechanisms for investor protection and the legal and regulatory framework (information standards and disclosure requirements) should be prioritised. Moreover, the self-protection for emerging market economies that want to avoid the distressing effects of financial crises which tend to be a liquidity crisis in nature is an increase in international liquidity. It includes three components. One is an avoidance of excessive short-term debt. Second is an accumulation of foreign exchange reserves. Third is the creation of a collaterized credit facility. Having large reserves and access to substantial additional foreign loans can enable a country to reduce the vulnerability and increase confidence in its currency. In addition, the countries with strong banking systems and good bank supervision like Singapore prevented the difficulties that occurred in the crisis countries.

It should be kept in mind that in order to achieve sustained and stable growth, countries should have a sound and stable macroeconomic environment and well-functioning and strong financial systems which are supported by a dynamic and adaptive policy regime. This regime should have the following characteristics: strong financial systems, sustained fiscal accounts, low inflation, credible and coherent monetary and exchange rate policies, moderate external and internal indebtedness, sustained current accounts, and adequate domestic saving rates.

Thailand has complied with most of the policy changes agreed with the IMF in the context of the 1997 rescue program. Since then, the situation has gradually improved. However, distressed assets of both the corporate sector and its financial sector counterpart remain high because the fundamentally complex microeconomic restructuring process takes time. As the large debt overhang still remains, the financial sector cannot fully play its role as financial intermediary in facilitating sustained economic growth. Also, the credit channel of monetary policy transmission was impaired after the crisis.

A flexible, market-based and case-by-case approach represents the best bet and the only realistic option for achieving financial stability and sustained growth (McDonough, 2003). Thailand is moving in this direction combined with its own way of problem solving and continuous financial sector restructuring towards international standards and best practices with an aim to prevent a similar crisis or to minimise losses if a crisis may occur in the future.

Appendix 2.A.1: Appendix Tables

Table 2.A.1.1: Summary of Theories Relating Financial Crises

Theories	Summary	Critiques
1) First generation model (fundamentalists) (for example: Krugman, 1979)	The collapse of exchange rate parity is an outcome of inconsistent monetary policy that leads to steady loss of international reserves	- They are subject to unique equilibrium and over simplistic. - There are often jumps in exchange rates. - How about government actions to eliminate deficit? - They cannot explain ERM crisis of 1992.
2) Second generation models (non-fundamentalists) (for example: Obstfeld, 1994)	The crises in foreign exchange market are owing to rational and self-fulfilling expectations which can be triggered by random phenomenon like sunspots.	- There are some paradoxes for example, the models explain that crisis can be occurred as a result of a self-fulfilling attacks triggered by random events, however, at the same time, the models present that because of deteriorated fundamentals, the economy would jump to the bad equilibrium and the crisis happens.
3) Third generation models (for example: Krugman, 1999)	The existing models have not mentioned three facets; contagion, the transfer problem and balance sheet problems. The model presents that the factors that can make financial collapse possible are: high leverage of entrepreneurs, low marginal propensity to import and large foreign-currency debt relative to exports.	Remark: - The world seems to keep finding new ways to generate crises.
4) Twin Crisis (for example: Glick and Hutchison, 1999 and Kaminsky and Reinhart, 1999)	The association of bank and currency crises and the occurrence of win crises may be attributable to three main channels of causation: a bank crisis leading to a currency crisis, a currency crisis leading to a bank crisis, or joint causality.	
5) Other non-conventional determinants; Crisis-Mania, Panic and Crash (Kindleberger, 1996), Market Euphoria, Contagion and Political factors	Kindleberger (1996, cited in Saqib, 2002) presents that there are three phases that lead to a financial crisis-mania, panic and crash. A focused model includes five different contemporaneous stages of displacement, boom, overtrading, revulsion, and tranquility. Market euphoria presents that most of the crises in recent times occurred after a prolonged period of economic boom.	- Crisis-mania, panic and crash model is overly broad and the causality between the different stages seem confusing, except for the very first and very last stages.

Source: Krugman, 1979, Obstfeld, 1994, Krugman, 1999, Glick and Hutchison, 1999, Kaminsky and Reinhart, 1999, Saqib, 2002 and Allen and Gale, 2003.

Table 2.A.1.2: Occurrences of Banking and Currency Crisis

No.	Country	Banking Crisis	Currency Crisis
	Industrial Countries		
1	Austria		
2	Belgium		1982
3	Canada	1983-1985	1976, 1992
4	Denmark	1987-1992	
5	Finland	1991-1994	1977-1978, 1982, 1991-93
6	France	1994-1995	1982
7	Germany	1978-1979	
8	Greece	1991-1995	1980, 1982-83, 1985
9	Iceland	1985-1986, 1993	1983-1984, 1988, 1992-93
10	Ireland		
11	Italy	1990-1995	1976, 1992, 1995
12	Japan	1992-1997	1979, 1989-1990
13	Luxembourg		
14	Netherlands		
15	New Zealand	1987-1990	1975, 1983-88, 1991
16	Norway	1987-1993	1978, 1986, 1992
17	Portugal	1986-1989	1976-1978, 1982-83, 1993, 1995
18	Spain	1977-1985	1976-1977, 1982, 1992-93
19	Sweden	1990-1993	1977, 1981-1982, 1992-93
20	Switzerland		1978
21	United Kingdom	1975-1976, 1984	1976, 1979, 1981-82, 1986, 1992
	Emerging Markets		
22	Argentina	1980-1982, 1989-1990, 1995-97	1975-1976, 1982-1983, 1989-1991
23	Bangladesh	1987-1996	1975-1976
24	Botswana	1994-1995	1984-1986, 1996
25	Brazil	1990, 1994-97	1982-1983, 1987, 1990-91, 1995
26	Chile	1976, 1981-83	1985
27	Colombia	1982-1987	1985
28	Ecuador	1980-1982, 1996-97	1982-1983, 1985-1986, 1988
29	Egypt	1980-1985, 1991-95	1979, 1989-1991
30	Hong Kong	1982-1986	
31	Ghana	1982-1989, 1997	1978, 1983, 1986-1987
32	India	1993-1997	1976, 1991, 1993, 1995
33	Indonesia	1994, 1997	1978, 1983, 1986, 1997
34	Jordan	1989-1990	1983, 1987-1989, 1992
35	Kenya	1985-1989, 1992-97	1975, 1981-82, 1985, 1993-95, 1997
36	Korea	1997	1980, 1997
37	Malaysia	1985-1988, 1997	1986, 1997
38	Mauritius	1996	1979, 1981
39	Mexico	1981-1991, 1995-97	1976, 1982, 1985, 1994-95
40	Morocco		1983-1985, 1990
41	Pakistan		
42	Peru	1983-1990	1976, 1979, 1978-88
43	Philippines	1981-1987, 1997	1983-1984, 1986, 1997
44	Singapore	1982	1975
45	South Africa	1977, 1985, 1989	1975, 1978, 1984-86, 1996
46	Sri Lanka	n.a.	n.a.
47	Thailand	1983-1987, 1997	1981, 1984, 1997

Table 2.A.1.2: Occurrences of Banking and Currency Crisis (continued)

Country	Banking Crisis	Currency Crisis
Emerging Markets		
48 Trinidad and Tobago	1982-93	1985, 1988, 1993
49 Tunisia	1991-95	1993
50 Turkey	1982-85, 1991, 1994-95	1978-80, 1994
51 Uruguay	1981-1984	1982-83
52 Venezuela	1978-86, 1994-97	1984, 1986, 1994-96
53 Zimbabwe	1995-97	1982, 1991, 1993-94, 1997
Other Developing		
54 Belize		
55 Bolivia	1986-87, 1994-97	1981-1985, 1988, 1990-91
56 Burundi	1994-97	1976, 1983, 1986, 1988-89, 1991, 1997
57 Cameroon	1987-93, 1995-97	1982, 1984, 1994
58 Costa Rica	1987, 1994-97	1981
59 Cyprus		
60 Dominican Republic		1985, 1987, 1990
61 El Salvador	1989	1986, 1990
62 Equatorial Guinea	1983-85	1991, 1994
63 Ethiopia	1994-95	1992
64 Fiji		1986-1987
65 Grenada		1978
66 Guatemala	1991-92	1986, 1989-1990
67 Guinea-Bissau	1995-97	1991, 1996
68 Guyana	1993-95	1978, 1989-1991
69 Haiti		1977, 1991
70 Honduras		1990
71 Hungary	1991-95	1989, 1994-1995
72 Jamaica	1994-97	1978, 1983-1984, 1990-1992
73 Lao P.D.R.	1991-94, 1997	1995
74 Madagascar	1988	1984, 1986-1987, 1991, 1994, 1996
75 Malawi		1982, 1985-1987, 1992, 1994
76 Mali	1987-89	1993
77 Malta		1992, 1997
78 Mozambique	1987-97	1993, 1995
79 Myanmar	1996-97	1975-1977
80 Nepal	1988-94	1975, 1981-1982, 1984-1986, 1991, 1993, 1995
81 Nicaragua	1988-96	1993
82 Nigeria	1993-1997	1986-1987, 1989, 1992
83 Panama	1988-1989	
84 Paraguay	1995-1997	1984-1986, 1988-1989, 1992
85 Romania	1990-1997	1990-1991
86 Sierra Leone	1990-1997	1988-1990, 1997
87 Swaziland	1995	1975, 1979, 1982, 1984-1986
88 Syrian Arab Rep.		1977, 1982, 1988
89 Uganda	1994-1997	1981, 1987-1989
90 Zambia	1995	1985, 1987, 1994

Source: Glick and Hutchison, 1999

Table 2.A.1.3: Threshold Values for Signalling Crises

Indicators	Threshold Values and the Location of the Critical Region: BOP Crises	Threshold Values and the Location of the Critical Region: Banking Crises	Comments
FINANCIAL LIBERALISATION			
M2 multiplier	>0.86	>0.90	Both banking and currency crises have been linked to rapid growth boom-bust) in credit and the monetary aggregates.
Domestic Credit/GD	>0.90	>0.95	
Real Interest Rate	>0.88	>0.80	For banking crises, the choice is umambigous since financial deregulation is associated with high interest rates (which could reflect increases risk taking. A liquidity crunch (say to defend a peg) will also hurt the banks. For balance of payments crises, it is less clear cut; higher real interest rates could reflect higher risk premium and fears of devaluation. Yet, using the lower interest rates for signals could be justified for balance-of-payments crises on the basis of loose monetary policy. An increase in the lending/deposit ratio can capture a decline in loan quality.
Lending-deposit rate ratio	>0.80	>0.87	
OTHER FINANCIAL			
Excess M1 balance	>0.94	>0.91	This is a loose monetary policy story.
M2/reserves	>0.87	>0.90	
Bank Deposits	<0.10	<0.16	Capital flight and a run against the domestic banks may precede both currency and banking crises.
EXTERNAL SECTOR			
CURRENT ACCOUNT			
Exports	<0.10	<0.10	Real exchange rate overvaluations and a weak external sector are a part of a currency crisis. It adds vulnerability of the banking sector, since a loss of competitiveness and external markets could lead to a recession, business failures, and a decline in the quality of loans. Thus, large negative shocks to exports, the terms of trade, and the real exchange rate are associated with signals.
Terms of Trade	<0.16	<0.19	
Real Exchange Rate	<0.10	<0.10	
Imports	>0.90	>0.80	Theory is ambiguous as to where we should locate the rejection region. Rapid import growth could be the sign of a buoyant economy (this would argue for a negative shock to imports); it could also be the sign of overvaluation, hence a positive shock could be a signal. Both possibilities are explored.
CAPITAL ACCOUNT			
Reserves	<0.15	<0.28	See discussion under bank deposits and real interest rates in Kaminsky and Reinhart, 1999.
Real interest rate differential	>0.89	>0.81	
REAL SECTOR			
Output	<0.11	<0.14	Recessions and the burst of asset price bubbles precede financial crises.
Stock prices	<0.11	<0.10	
FISCAL SECTOR			
Deficit/GDP	>0.86	>0.86	Loose fiscal policy financed by credit from the central bank.

Source: Kaminsky and Reinhart, 1999
Note: The definitions and sources of the indicator are described below.

The Indicators
Sources: International Financial Statistics (IFS), International Monetary Fund (IMF); Emerging Market Indicators, International Finance Corporation (IFC); World Development Indicators, the World Bank (WB). When data was missing from these sources, central bank bulletins and other country-specific sources were used as supplements. Unless otherwise noted, we used 12-month percent changes.
1. M2 Multiplier: The ratio of M2 (IFS lines 34 plus 35) to base money (IFS line 14)
2. Domestic Credit/GDP: IFS line 52 divided by IFS line 64 to obtain domestic credit in real terms, which was then divided by IFS line 99b.p (interpolated) to obtain the domestic credit/GDP ratio. Monthly real GDP was interpolated from annual data.
3. Real Interest Rate: Deposit rate (IFS line 60) deflated using consumer prices (IFS line 64). Monthly rates expressed in percentage points. (in levels)
4. Lending-Deposit rate ratio: IFS line 60p divided by IFS line 60 was used in lieu of differential to ameliorate the distortions caused by the large percentage point spreads observed during high inflation. (in levels)
5. "Excess" M1 balances: M1 (IFS line 34) deflated by consumer prices (IFS line 64) less an estimated demand for money. The demand for real balances is determined by real GDP (interpolated IFS line 99b.p), domestic consumer price inflation, and a time trend. Domestic inflation was used in lieu of nominal interest rates, as market determined interest rates were not available during the entire sample for a number of countries; the time trend (which can enter log-linearly, linearly, or exponentially) is motivated by its role as a proxy for financial innovation and/or currency substitution. (in levels)
6. M2/Reserves: IFS lines 34 plus 35 converted into dollars (using IFS line ae) divided by IFS line 1L.d.
7. Bank deposits: IFS line 24 plus 25 deflated by consumer prices (IFS line 64)
8. Exports: IFS line 70
9. Imports: IFS line 71
10. Terms of Trade: The unit value of exports (IFS line 74) over the unit value of imports (IFS line 75). For those developing countries where import unit values (or import price indices) were not available, an index of prices of manufactured exports from industrial countries to developing countries was used.
11. The real exchange rate: The real exchange rate index is derived from a nominal exchange rate index, adjusted for relative consumer prices (IFS line 64). The measure is defined as the relative price of foreign goods (in domestic currency) to the price of domestic goods. The nominal exchange rate index is a weighted average of the exchange rates of the nineteen OECD countries with weights equal to the country trade shares with the OECD countries. Since not all real appreciations reflect disequilibrium phenomena, we focus on deviations of the real exchange rate from trend. The trend was specified as, alternatively, log, linear, and exponential; the best fit among these was selected on a country-by-country basis. (in levels)
12. Reserves: IFS line 1L.d.
13. Real interest rate differential: Interest rates in the domestic economy are compared with interest rates in the United States (Germany) if the domestic central bank pegs the currency to the dollar (Deutsche mark). The interest rate differential is constructed as the difference between real rates for the domestic and foreign countries. Real rates are deposit rates (IFS line 60) deflated using consumer prices (IFS line 64).
14. Output: For most countries, the measure of output used is industrial production (IFS line 66). However, for some countries, (the commodity exporters) an index of output of primary commodities is used (IFS lines 66aa), if industrial production is not available.
15. Stock returns: IFC global indices are used for all emerging markets; for industrial countries the quotes from the main boards are used. All stock prices are in US dollars.
16. GDP: Consolidated public sector deficit as a share of GDP. World Development Indicators.

Source: Kaminsky and Reinhart, 1999

Table 2.A.1.4: Thailand's Basic Economic Data during 1996-2002

Indicators	1996	1997	1998	1999	2000	2001	2002
	(Annual percentage change, unless otherwise indicated)						
1. National Accounts and Prices							
1.1 Real GDP	5.9	-1.4	-10.5	4.4	4.6	1.8	5.2
1.2 Nominal GDP	10.1	2.6	-2.2	0.1	5.9	4.0	6.0
1.3 Nominal GDP (in billions of baht)	4,611.0	4,732.6	4,626.4	4,632.1	4,904.7	5,099.6	5,430.5
1.4 GDP deflator	4.0	4.1	9.2	-4.1	1.2	2.1	0.7
1.5 Consumer prices (average)	5.9	5.5	8.1	0.3	1.6	1.7	0.6
1.6 Unemployment rate	1.5	1.5	4.4	4.2	3.6	3.3	2.4
	(Annual percentage change, unless otherwise indicated)						
2. Money and Credit 1/							
2.1 Money and quasi-money(M2a)(end of period)	12.7	2.0	2.1	1.3	3.5	4.7	2.4
Stock in percent of GDP	1.0	1.0	1.1	1.1	1.1	1.1	1.0
2.2 Domestic credit 2/	13.9	34.5	-1.2	-4.2	-7.4	-6.1	7.8
Credit to private sector 3/	14.4	30.5	-7.9	-5.7	-8.5	-7.5	8.5
Non-performing loans (% of total loans at year end) 2/	n.a.	n.a.	45.0	38.9	17.7	10.4	15.6
	(Annual percentage change, unless otherwise indicated)						
3. Interest rates and exchange rates							
3.1 Overnight interbank rate	12.1	21.7	2.6	1.2	1.7	2.1	1.6
3.2 Minimum lending rates (Avg. of five largest banks)	13.1	15.3	11.8	8.4	7.9	7.3	6.8
3.3 Baht/US dollar(average of period)	25.3	31.4	41.4	37.8	40.2	44.5	43.0
3.4 Nominal effective exchange rate (1994=100)	98.6	88.1	72.0	75.2	72.0	68.2	70.4
3.5 Real effective exchange rate (1994)=100)	104.7	96.5	83.7	86.8	83.4	79.5	81.7
3.6 Term of trade (deterioration -)	n/a	0.5	-5.9	1.3	-8.9	-9.4	-1.5
	(in billions of U.S. Dollar)						
4. Balance of Payments 2/							
4.1 Export	54.7	56.7	52.9	56.8	67.9	63.2	66.8
% change	-1.9	3.8	-6.8	7.4	19.5	-6.9	5.7
4.2 Import	70.8	61.3	40.7	47.5	62.4	60.7	63.4
% change	0.6	-13.4	-33.8	16.9	31.3	-2.8	4.4
4.3 Trade balance	-16.1	-4.6	12.2	9.3	5.5	2.5	3.4
4.4 Current account balance	-14.3	-3.1	14.3	12.5	9.3	6.2	7.6
% of GDP	-7.9	-2.0	12.7	10.2	7.6	5.4	6.0
4.5 Net Capital Movement	19.5	-4.3	-9.8	-7.9	-10.3	-4.8	-4.0
Private (including commerical banks and BIBFs)	18.2	-7.6	-15.5	-13.5	-9.8	-4.1	-5.5
Public	1.3	1.6	1.8	1.6	-0.3	-0.3	-2.5
Bank of Thailand	-	1.7	3.9	4.0	-0.2	-0.4	4.0
4.6 Balance of payments	2.2	-10.6	1.7	4.6	-1.6	1.3	4.2
4.7 Swap Obligations		18.0	6.6	4.8	2.1	2.1	0.5
	(in billions of U.S. Dollar)						
5. International Reserves and externa debt 3/							
5.1 International reserves	38.7	27.0	29.5	34.8	32.7	33.0	38.9
In months of imports	6.6	5.3	8.7	8.8	6.3	6.5	7.4
5.2 Oustanding external debt	108.7	109.3	105.1	95.0	79.7	67.3	58.9
of which: public debt	16.8	24.1	31.6	36.2	33.9	28.3	23.3
of which: private debt	47.7	38.3	28.3	19.4	14.7	13.2	11.5
5.3 Ratio of gross reserves to private s-t debt (%)	81.2	70.5	104.5	179.2	222.7	249.9	338.1

Sources : IMF, 2003 and Bank of Thailand, 2003

Notes: 1/ Excludes data from 56 closed finance companies. 2/ from Bank of Thailand 3/ End of period.

Appendix 2.A.2: How were Crises alike or Different?

Bordo and Eichengreen (2002) studied banking and currencies crises in 21 countries that occurred in the pre-1914 period (1880-1913), the interwar years (1919-1939), the Bretton Woods period (1945-1971), and the post Bretton Woods era (1973-1998). They also included larger sample of 56 countries starting in 1973 because of a significant increase in the number of candidate countries. They concentrated on the comparison of crisis problems that occurred between the two eras of globalisation, pre-1914 period and 1973-1998. Their main finding is that crises are growing more frequent but not more severe. During 1880-1998, crises were followed by economic slowdowns lasting on averaged about 2-3 years and costing 5-10 percent of GDP. The recent crises (1973-1998) were similar to the crises in the pre-1914 period (1880-1913) in important respects. Speed of recovery from currency crises is faster today whereas the speed of recovery from banking and twin crises is slower (Allen, 2003).

Taking account of all crises, as to the frequency, compared to the pre-1914 period of financial globalisation, crises in 1973-1998 doubled, resulting from the growing occurrence of currency crises. On the other hand, the frequency of banking crises was roughly the same between pre-1914 and 1973-1998 periods. Consequently, a growing frequency of twin crises was observed. One of the explanations of the stability of the pre-1914 financial environment is the credibility of the commitment to peg the exchange rate under the gold standard. As to the severity, there is little evidence that the output losses from crises are growing or that time for recovery is lengthening (Bordo and Schwartz, 2000 and Bordo and Eichengreen , 2002).

Table 2.2.1 Summary of the Financial Crises during 1880-1998

No.	Periods	Main Characteristics
1	Gold Standard Era (1880-1913)	The crises were not typically caused by chronic government budget deficits. On the other hand, crises originated in the private sector, in general, in inefficient managed, regulated banking systems and in the boom and bust of real estate and property market.
2	Interwar Period (1919-1939)	Banking and currency crises were widespread. The output losses caused by the crises were remarkably large.
3	Bretton Woods Period (1945-1971)	The regulations of bank balance sheets were prevalent. Consequently, there were no banking crises or twin crises.
4	Recent Period (1973-1998)	Following the collapse of the Bretton Woods system of fixed exchange rates in the early 1970s, banking crises and twin crises re-emerged since financial environment moved back towards global capital markets. Crises occurred in both developed countries like Norway, Finland, Sweden and Japan and developing countries. The crises were most like the crises in the Gold Standard Era (1880-1913).

Sources: Bordo and Schwartz, 1996 and 2002, Bordo and Eichengreen, 2002 and Allen, 2003.

Appendix 2.A.3: The Calculation of the Resource Balance Gap

The criterion of solvency can be made operational by calculating the `resource balance gap´. In a country where the debt to GDP ratio is growing, the gap is the difference between the current trade balance and the trade surplus required to stabilise the debt to GDP ratio in the long run. The gap can be larger for the countries with a large trade deficit to GDP ratio, a large debt to GDP ratio, or a large differential between the real interest rate and the growth rate of the economy.

From the current account identity

$B_{t+1} = (1+r) B_t - T_t$

where B is the net debt position of the country and T is the trade balance and divide both sides by current GDP, denoted Y_t

Assuming that GDP grows at the constant rate g, so that $Y_{t+1} / Y_t = 1+g$, then, the previous expression can be written as

$$(1+g) b_{t+1} = (1+r) b_t - \tau_t$$

where $b = B/Y$ and $\tau = \frac{T}{Y}$ For the debt to GDP ratio to be constant in the long run at the same level b, the trade balance surplus (as a fraction of GDP) must be equal to (r-g)b. The resource balance gap is the difference between the above trade surplus and the currently observed trade balance (both as percentage of GDP).

Source: Corsetti et al., 1998a, p. 9

Appendix 2.A.4: The Background of the Thai Economy

A. Performance in 1995-1996

Notwithstanding a strong reserve position and macroeconomic performance, the Thai baht also came under speculative pressures in early 1995. Speculation prove short-lived, however, as the authorities intervened to keep the peg in place. A reserve loss of US $ 375 million in January was sufficient to restore confidence. Stock price, measured in dollars, remained unaffected by the events in Mexico and elsewhere. After a slight drop, the index began to recover.

B. Performance in 1997 (the crisis year)

The Thai economy faced severe difficulties in 1997, mainly as result of the bubble economy, which made the country highly dependent on short-term foreign capital and overly exposed to unproductive and speculative investment in the asset markets.

The structural problems of slackening productivity and eroding export competitiveness led to an export slump in 1996 and the modest recovery in the first half of 1997. As a result, the current account deficit remained high; the economic slowdown reached an extent far beyond anticipation.

The economic problems largely affected market confidence, leading to chronic currency speculation that persisted throughout the first half of 1997 and obliged the Bank of Thailand to intervene in the foreign exchange market as deemed necessary. It was insufficient to regain the confidence in the baht and foreign capital outflow continued.

The marked economic slowdown started to affect the performance of financial institutions. The problem of non-performing loans (NPLs) provoked the loss of both creditors' and depositors' confidence in a number of finance companies, 16 of which were temporarily suspended on June 26, to ease market panic. On July 2, the authority abandoned the basket-pegged exchange rate system and replaced it with managed floating exchange rate system.

Credit rating agencies downgraded the country's foreign currency bonds on several occasions. The baht depreciated largely while the liquidity problem in several financial institutions became increasingly severe. The authority announced the temporary suspension of 42 additional financial companies on August 5, and sought both financial and technical assistance from the IMF, the stand-by arrangement of US$ 4 billion altogether with other international organizations and central banks; the rescue package amounted to US$17.2 billion.

C. Performance in 1998-2000 (the period of post-crisis)

In 1998, the sharp contraction in domestic demand, particularly private consumption and investment in line with the fall in real income, increased unemployment and excess production capacity; decline in wealth and debt overhang; prevailing uncertainty and risk, as well as credit crunch. A sharp decline brought by contraction in demand together with improved export performance resulted in the robust current account surplus. The moderation in capital outflows contributed to the overall balance of payment surplus, strengthening of international reserves and the decline of external debt with the lengthening of maturity profile. However, the financial system remained subject to risk and uncertainty.

In 1999, the improved economic performance with economic growth of 4.2 percent due mainly to the increased domestic demand as a result of fiscal stimulus measures. Inflation rate for the year averaged at 0.3 percent despite the pressure from the rising oil prices in the world market. Low inflation allowed the interest rates to continue to decline, which supported the corporate debt restructuring. The current account recorded surplus. Private sector's external debt declined with lengthening of maturity profile. Liquidity remained high enabled the interest rates in the money market to fall.

In the second half of 2000, the economic recovery begun in 1999 softened somewhat. Lower domestic demand was caused by higher oil prices and low equity prices, which weakened consumers' confidence. Fiscal stimulus was eased while bank lending did not resume their normal pace despite the fact that the NPLs problem had been partially resolved.

Source: Radelet and Sachs, (1998) and Bank of Thailand's Annual Report 1998, 1999 and 2000.

Appendix 2.A.5: The Financial Sector Reform during the Post-Crisis

During the 1997 financial crisis, Thai economy contracted and banks faced severe liquidity shortages and a sharp deterioration in the quality of their assets. In order to reform and rehabilitate the financial system, the authorities have implemented the following measures:

(A) The aim of strengthening financial systems

1. Closure of Finance Companies and Establishment of the Financial Sector Restructuring Authority (FRA) and the Asset Management Corporation (AMC)

1.1 Closure of 56 Finance Companies

Prior to the 1997 crisis, 91 finance companies operated in Thailand, providing banking services to individual consumers. On June 27, 1997, the operations of 16 insolvent and liquidity-strapped finance companies were suspended. On August 5, 1997, an additional 42 finance companies become insolvent and had their license suspended. The authorities arranged a compensation scheme for bearers of promissory notes or certificates of deposit issues by the 58 finance companies whose operations had been suspended. The scheme involved Financial Institutions Development Fund (FIDF) brokered exchange of promissory notes and certificates of deposit issued by the 58 finance companies for certificates of deposit issued by selected commercial banks.

On December 8, 1997, the Government made an announcement to allow only 2 of the 58 suspended finance companies to resume business. The remaining 56 companies, with total assets of about 860 billion Baht or 10.68% of the financial sector, were closed and liquidated under the supervision of the Financial Sector Restructuring Authority (FRA).

1.2 The Financial Sector Restructuring Authority (FRA)

FRA was established on October 24, 1997 as an independent organization under the Ministry of Finance. Its responsibility was to review the rehabilitation plans of 58 suspended finance companies and to oversee the liquidation process and to safeguard the interests of bona fide depositors and creditors of the suspended companies.

1.3 The Asset Management Corporation (AMC)

AMC was set up in November 1997 as an independent government body and its purpose is to act as a bidder of last resort for the impaired assets of the 56 finance companies auctioned by the FRA.

2. The Blanket Guarantee of Depositors and Creditors

Despite the closure of 58 suspended finance companies in 1997, withdrawal of funds from the remaining finance companies continued unabated and threatened to spread to the rest of the financial systems. To stop the crisis, the Government announced on August 5, 1997 a blanket guarantee, in local currency terms, for both depositors and creditors of domestic and foreign financial institutions operating in Thailand. The guarantee, implemented through the stated-owned Financial Institutions Development Fund (FIDF), applied only to financial institutions which had not been closed or had not ceased making payments, and it covered full principal and full or (under certain conditions) partial interest amount. The public panic was thus contained.

3. August 14 Financial Restructuring Package

The government announced a comprehensive financial restructuring package on August 14, 1998. The package focused on three main aspects as follows: Intervention, Merger and Privatisation of Weak Institutions: During 1997-1998, 7 banks and 69 finance companies were intervened. Resolution strategies for the intervened financial institutions were based on the following objectives: be cost-efficient, facilitate consolidation of the banking sector, ensure credibility and transparency, enhance confidence in the banking system and ensure consistency with the capital support facilities. In solving the problem banks, the authority attempted to resolve the problems using a least-cost approach. A capital write-down would first be ordered, thus forcing the existing shareholders to bear the loss prior to the injection of new capital by the FIDF Recapitalisation Scheme: The capital support scheme of the Ministry of Finance (MOF) was aimed at strengthening the financial system by providing funds to assist the recapitalisation of viable financial institutions, which would enable them to make loans. There are two types of recapitalisation facilities:

Tier-1 Capital Support Facility: A financial institution applying to tier-1 capital support was required to immediately adopt, and implement, full Loan Classification and Provisioning (LCP) rules, without benefit of the phase in period. Capital injections under this facility took the form of placement of 10 years government bonds. The government, in turn, would acquire preferred shares of the applying financial institution, in an amount sufficient to raise the BIS tier-1 ratio to 2.5%.

Tier-2 Capital Support Facility: The amount of tier-2 capital support depended on the amount of loss resulting from debt restructuring, net of previous provision and the size of additional new lending. Capital injections under this facility were in the form of government bonds in exchange for bank's qualified subordinated debts.

Private Asset Management Company (AMC): Many financial institutions were unable to raise fresh capital or grant credits due to their high level of NPLs. Transferring the NPLs to an AMC could mitigate these problems.

4. Corporate Debt Restructuring

In 1998 and 1999 the BOT took many related actions to promote corporate debt restructuring for example, issued regulations on debt restructuring, asset classification, and collateral valuation, developed and improved reporting systems for debt restructuring, NPLs and classified assets, and established the Corporate Debt Restructuring Advisory Committee (CDRAC) to set policies and guidelines, monitor and facilitate and expedite corporate debt restructuring.

5. Relaxation of Restrictions on Foreign Ownership

On June 27, 1997 the Government issued an Emergency Decree amending the commercial Banking Act B.E. 2505 (1962) (No. 2). The Emergency Decree relaxed existing restrictions on the foreign ownership of commercial banks by allowing 100% shareholding for foreign investors who step in to resolve or rehabilitate financial institutions, subject to certain conditions. Specifically, foreign investors are permitted to acquire a majority ownership interest in locally-incorporated financial institutions for a period of 10 years, following which additional shares may not be acquired until the ownership interest (both existing and new holdings) are maintained at 49% of total shares outstanding or less.

(B) The aim of improving governance and transparency

6. Fit and Proper Criteria for Management

Additional guidelines were issued on November 28, 1997, requiring top executives of restricted-licensed bank to have at least 5 years experience in high-level positions and in the management and administration of well run financial institutions. In addition, a further notification of the BOT was issued to prohibit board members or commercial bank executives from serving as a broad member in more than 3 other companies.

7. The Establishment of Credit Bureau

The establishment of a credit bureau was included in the 5-year Financial System Master Plan (March 1, 1995 –February 29, 2000). However, the establishment of Credit Bureau has not been finalised.

8. Good Corporate Governance

The BOT has put forth various measures relating to the practice of good corporate governance for example, Transparency; financial institutions are required to disclose information on NPLs and lending to related parties and Sound lending practices; bank's lending to related companies with cross-directorship is restricted.

(C) The aim of restoring economic competitiveness

9. The provision of Incentive Package for Merger and Acquisition

The Notification of the MOF dated December 28, 1998 was issued to allow the establishment of restricted-licensed bank through merger or acquisition of at least 5 entities of finance companies, finance and securities companies and credit foncier companies with good track records and stable financial standing.

(D) The aim of modernising the legal and regulatory environment

10. The Supervision Standards Upgrade New policies and procedures include guidelines on accruing interest income, asset valuation, loan review, asset classification and provisioning. These regulatory changes were announced in June 1998 and became effective for the accounting period ending on December 31, 1998.

Source: Bank of Thailand (2001) and grouped according to the aims of the IMF programme.

Chapter 3 Cost Efficiency of Domestic and Foreign Banks in Thailand

3.1 Introduction

Thailand experienced massive changes since the 1997 twin crisis, the worst recorded in its economic history. After 10 years (1987-1996) of stable and rapid economic and financial development, in 1997 the Thai economy experienced a severe twin crisis, which is a simultaneous crisis in the balance of payments and in the banking system (Glick and Hutchison, 1999 and Kaminsky and Reinhart, 1999). There is a close link between a country's currency stability and the health of its banking sector. Devaluation negatively affects the balance sheets of financial intermediaries, which leads to a tightening in credit market conditions and possibly to a contraction in output. In addition, the adverse effects of devaluation are worse if banks' balance sheets are deteriorated by non-performing loans (NPLs), or if banks borrow heavily in foreign currencies, particularly short term. As a result, banking and currency crises can amplify each other (Pesenti and Tille, 2000 and Kaminsky and Reinhart, 1999).

Before the onset of the 1997 twin crisis, Thailand's banks were regarded as a positive element in the economy, and Thailand was classified as one of the group of the 'East Asian miracle' countries which had notably improved in total factor productivity (World Bank, 1993). Although banks in emerging economies are weaker than those in industrialised countries, in terms of capital base, performance and regulations, it does not seem likely that they are inefficient in resource management (Bhagwati, 2002 and Menkhoff and Suwanaporn, 2003). Thai banks have not performed worse than any other bank in other countries, both in terms of allocative efficiency and operational efficiency (Menkhoff and Suwanaporn, 2003). However, it seems that a large number of Thai financial institutions were distressed by the first half of 1997. What went wrong in the Thai banking sector and made the positive performance disappear within a few years? One possible answer to this question is that financial liberalisation was rushed and the authorities did not pay sufficient attention to the fact that the capital market is difficult to monitor than the goods market (Bhagwati, 2002).

Currency and banking crises are not a new episode. International economic crises will probably continue to occur in the future as they have for centuries. Emerging market countries which want to avoid the devasting effects of such crises should create efficient early warning systems, associated with standard country surveillance, reduce the vulnerability of their economies by getting macroeconomic policies right, and create sound banking, increasing international liquidity and shifting toward risk-based incentives to supervision regulations (Feldstein, 1999 and 2000 and Kawai et al., 2001).

After the crisis, Thailand has complied with most of the policy changes agreed with the IMF in the context of the 1997 rescue program. However, distressed assets of both the corporate sector and its financial sector counterpart have remained high. Because of the large debt overhang, the financial sector has not fully played its role as financial intermediary in facilitating sustained economic growth. Also, the credit channel of monetary policy transmission was impaired after the crisis. Hence, a close examination of bank performance, in particular in different groups of banks, is important for research and policy. This will contribute to handling and preventing crises and will be of use also for policy making relating to banking competition.

From a historical point of view, banking has been a heavily regulated industry in most countries. Consequently, the interest in studying bank efficiency and changes therein stems from a desire to know how deregulation and liberalisation affects the industry. For instance, in the US there used to be regulations which restricted banks in their ability to open branches outside their home state and regulations restricting commercial banks in their ability to enter investment banking etc. Early studies on banking efficiency for instance suggested that the minimum efficient scale for banks is fairly large; this implied that regulations which prevented banks from operating outside their home state often forced banks to operate below efficient scale, and that deregulation would improve efficiency. Recent studies tried to check whether deregulation did increase competition and improve efficiency. Similar efforts have been made to examine whether increases in foreign bank participation when markets were liberalized would increase competition and efficiency (Berger and Mester, 1997, Berger and Humphrey, 1997, Goldberg et al., 2000, Clarke et al., 2001, Sturm and Williams, 2004 and Detragiache and Gupta, 2004).

Banking efficiency research has been conducted extensively for U.S. commercial banks, to a smaller extent for European financial institutions and relatively little for Asian financial institutions (Kwan, 2003 and Berger and Hamphrey, 1997). There have also been only few studies comparing efficiency between domestic and foreign banks in one country.

Bank efficiency studies can be classified into those which examine scale and scope efficiency alone, and those which also examine X-efficiency[1]. Most studies focus on scale and scope efficiency. The scale and scope studies estimate an average practice cost function which explains bank cost to output levels and input prices. The technique fundamentally assumes that there is no X-inefficiency and banks use the same production technology. In this setting, inefficiently high costs can arise if banks fail to operate at the efficient scale, or

[1] Scale efficiency – whether banks are operating with the efficiency level of outputs; scope efficiency – whether banks are operating with the efficiency mix of outputs; and X-efficiency – whether banks are using their inputs efficiently (Mester, 1996, p. 1026).

if they fail to operate with efficient scope, i.e. with an efficient output mix. On the other hand, X-efficiency studies estimate a best practice cost function, which represents the predicted cost function of banks that are X-efficient, and then assesses the degree of inefficiency of banks in the sample relative to this best practice technology[2] (Mester, 1996). Hence in addition to the above sources of inefficiency, inefficiently high costs can arise in this setting also from banks failing to use the efficient production technology or input mix. The present study focuses on X-efficiency and compares domestic and foreign banks in Thailand.

Instead of via the cost function, scale, scope or X-efficiency can in principle also be measured via the profit function. The reasons why most studies, including the present one, focus on cost efficiency can be classified into three main categories as asserted by Fries and Taci (2004) as follows. Firstly, stronger relative cost efficiency mostly comes along with the structural and institutional reforms. Secondly, greater cost efficiency or efficiency gains decrease the operating costs in both operations of payments systems and intermediation of savings into investments, which finally benefit the overall economic development. Thirdly, cost efficiency may be an advantage for other dimensions of bank performance which contribute to overall economic development, for instance, the identification of more productive lending opportunities. In addition, cost efficiency is one of the three common performance dimensions (the other two are capital adequacy and loan management) for identifying problem banks (Rahman et al., 2004).

Recently, the Bank of Thailand imposed the Financial Sector Master Plan, aiming at improving efficiency, stability and competition in the financial system and broadening accessibility of financial services to all potential users. In order to realise greater efficiency and less duplication of functions, under the restructuring the Thai financial institutions, there will be two types of licences to financial institutions that take deposits from the public: commercial banks and retail banks[3]. With reference to the restructuring of foreign-owned financial institutions, there will be two types of foreign bank licenses: subsidiaries of foreign banks and full branches of foreign banks (BOT, 2004). In summary, the study of cost efficiency of banks will enable policy makers to pinpoint current

---

[2] Three common methodologies are data envelopment analysis (DEA), thick frontier analysis, and stochastic econometric cost frontier analysis. None of these methodologies work without problem. (Mester, 1996).

[3] Commercial banks are banks with qualified and well capitalised which provide financial services to all groups of customers and carry out all types of financial transactions, except insurance underwriting as well as brokering, trading and underwriting of equity securities. Retail banks are banks with qualified and smaller capital requirement which offer financial services to retail customers and SMEs subject to exposure limits per customer and other conditions set by the BOT (BOT, 2004).

infrastructure weaknesses and promptly issue appropriate policy measures to cure such conditions.

The purposes of this paper are as follows:

1) To analyse the development of per unit operating costs of the banking industry in Thailand and to compare the cost efficiency of domestic and foreign banks in order to shed light on the cost advantages (if any) of foreign banks. The findings will have implications for regulatory policies relating to the size and competitiveness of domestic banks and foreign bank entry.

2) To examine the choice of input combination, for example, the combination of labour and physical capital in banking production across the different types of banks.

3) To investigate the effect of foreign bank entry on banking efficiency in Thailand after the significant acquisitions by banks from developed countries in 1999.

The rest of the paper is organised as follows. Section 3.2 provides the institutional background. Section 3.3 presents a review of the literature. Section 3.4 discusses the data descriptive analysis and the methodology. Section 3.5 shows the analysis of empirical results and section 6 provides concluding remarks.

3.2. Institutional Background

3.2.1 The Development of the Thai Banking Industry

Thailand's financial system is deep compared to other emerging market economies with similar per capita income. In fact, at the end-2002, total financial assets stood at about 158 percent of GDP (IMF, 2004). Most of the financial deepening took place at the beginning of the 1980s and was mainly due to an increasingly large share of private savings which was channelled into accumulation of financial assets. The Thai system is bank-oriented with limited financial intermediation through mutual funds and other type of institutional investors (Alba et al., 1999).

Thailand's financial system includes four main constituents: commercial banks, capital markets (consisting of both stock and bond markets), government-owned specialised financial institutions (SFIs) and non-bank financial intermediaries (finance companies, credit foncier companies, life insurance companies, and various financial co-operatives). Commercial banks are the oldest and largest part of the Thai financial system (Disyatat and Nakornthab, 2003) (see also table 2.3). Thailand's banking industry is characterised by an oligopolistic market structure. It seems that this oligopolistic structure and the lack of a threat of new entry obstructed innovation and diversification in the financial system (Alba et al., 1999). At end of 2002, commercial banks' assets stood at 106 percent of GDP, compared to 14 percent of GDP in 1960 (IMF, 2004).

On the other hand, bond and stock markets remain in the process of development. The value of all bonds outstanding increased from 12 percent of GDP at end-1997 to 42 percent of GDP at end-2002. As for Thailand's main equity market, at the peak in 1993 the Stock Exchange of Thailand (SET) market capitalisation stood at 105 percent of GDP. However, after the 1997 financial crisis, the SET market capitalisation has been relatively small despite recent gains, compared to other stock exchanges in the region. As of June-2003, the SET market capitalisation accounted for 47 percent of GDP (Disyatat and Nakornthab, 2003). Finance companies which have rather limited roles[4] tend to seek profits by allocating a major share of their portfolio into high risk areas, namely construction and real estate, leasing and personal consumption loans because of relative advantages of commercial banks in term of cost of funds and regulations (Alba et al., 1999). Finance companies were strongly affected by the 1997 financial crisis. At the peak at end-1996, finance companies assets stood at about one-third of those of commercial banks. Since the financial crisis, the number of finance companies decreased from 91 to 19 and their assets accounted for only one-seventh of their assets level in 1996 (Disyatat and Nakornthab, 2003).

3.2.2 Reform of the Thai Banking Sector

The financial liberalisation which took place in the late 1980s and early 1990s increased competition in the financial sector. The financial liberalisation programme had four main components: to deregulate the financial system; to develop financial instruments; to improve the payments system; and to improve the supervision and examination of financial institutions. The three main objectives of the programme were as follows: to increase competition in the domestic financial sector with the ultimate goal of improving the efficiency of savings mobilisation and credit allocation; to expand the financial sector for supporting economic expansion; and to establish Bangkok as the leading offshore financial centre[5] in the region. Financial liberalisation was carried

---

[4] Unlike commercial banks, finance and securities companies are not allowed to take direct deposits from the public. They fund their operations primarily through the issuance of promissory notes, credits from commercial banks, and funding from other financial institutions respectively. At the same time, like commercial banks, the largest share of finance companies' income comes from lending activities, followed by hire purchase business, securities trading, dividends on investments and other sources (Alba et al., 1999).

[5] The Bangkok International Banking Facilities (BIBFs) was established in 1993 with an aim of simplifying access to international capital in response to the I-S gap. There are two types of BIBF transactions. The first is out-out transactions which deal with taking deposits and lending in foreign currencies for specific activities overseas. The second is out-in transactions

out through a series of three-year financial system development plans[6] (Intarachote and Williams, 2003).

Table 3.1 presents the regulatory situation both before and after the financial liberalisation. One of the effects of financial liberalisation was that Thai banks developed new lines of business, in particular in the areas of investment banking and asset management. Moreover, domestic banks and corporations reduced their financing costs by raising relatively cheap funds from international financial markets. After financial liberalisation, the stock market rapidly boomed. In fact, between 1986 and 1993, the ratio of domestic banks' deposits to total domestic financial assets declined from 70.8 percent to 36.8, while the stock market's share increased from 8.6 percent to 51.2 percent during the same period (Intarachote and Williams, 2003). Because of relatively high interest rates in Thailand, BIBF's activities led to a greater influx of foreign capital, and such foreign capital competed with domestic banks for domestic business more than the Bank of Thailand expected. Moreover, liberalisation allowed commercial banks to focus less on lending and more on lucrative fee-based services, for example, advising, providing information, selling unit trusts, acting as trustees for mutual funds and bonds, as well as providing custodial services (Leightner and Lovell, 1998).

An analysis based on data for the period of 1989-1994 suggested that Thai financial liberalisation had been successful despite the fact that it carried high risks which needed to be carefully monitored (Leightner and Lovell, p. 129, 1998). In contrast, financial fragility increased from the mid-1990s because of technical regress and a declining efficiency. In fact, in the deregulated environment of the 1990s, profit efficiency declined at an increasing rate over time. On average, Thai banks lost 2.66 and 38.5 percent of potential profits to inefficiency in 1990 and 1997, respectively (Intarachote and Williams, 2003). On the other hand, foreign banks performed little better with efficiency losses of 2.62 and 37.69 percent, respectively.

---

which relate to foreign currency borrowings from overseas or other BIBFs, then to be on-lent in foreign currencies to the domestic sector.

[6] The first plan (1990-1992) increased competition and efficiency in the banking system which included the policies aiming to abolish interest rate restrictions, relaxing capital and foreign exchange controls, and extend the activities of banks and other domestic financial institutions. The second plan (1993-1995) enhanced savings mobilisation, expanded financial services to rural areas and developed Bangkok as a regional financial centre. The plan consisted of many policies targeting the strengthening of bank supervision, relaxing reserve requirements and entry barriers, and further deregulation of foreign exchange and capital control. The third plan (1996-1998) included the policies relating to the further deregulation of foreign exchange controls and relaxation of entry barriers into the domestic financial sector (Intarachote and Williams, 2003).

Table 3.1: Financial Liberalisation and Regulatory Change, 1990-1997

Regulation	*Pre-liberalisation*	*Post-liberalisation*	*Year*
A: STRUCTURE AND CONDUCT RULES			
1. Entry of new banks			
1.1 Thai banks	Moratorium since 1978	Permitted	1996
1.2 Foreign Banks	Moratorium since 1978	Entry under BIBF license	1993
		Full branch status	1996
2. Branching expansion			
2.1 Thai banks	16% bond holding requirement	Abolished	1993
2.2 Foreign Banks	Restricted	Permitted for a sound bank	1996
3. Interest rate ceilings			
3.1 Deposit rates	Controlled by the BOT	Free to set	1989-1992
		Temporarily controlled	1997
3.2 Lending rates	Controlled by the BOT	Set to BOT guidelines 1/	1992
4. Entry of new banking activities			
4.1 BIBF		License required	1993
4.2 Credit cards		Directly	1994
4.3 Underwriting and trading of debt instruments		Approval required	1992
4.4 Mutual funds		License required	1992
4.5 Portfolio requirement for Thai banks branches	Credit equal to at least 60% of deposits in each province	Credit equal to at least 60% of deposits in each province	1991
B: PRUDENTIAL AND SUPERVISORY RULES			
1. Capital requirement	8% of total assets	BIS standard Foreign banks tier 1 ratio to be at least equal to 6%	1993
2. Foreign exchange exposure	15% of tier 1 capital (liabilities)	Reduced to 10%	1993
	20% of tier 1 capital (assets)	Reduced to 15%	1993
3. Provision: doubtful debt	50% of doubtful assets	Increased to 100%	1994-1995
4. Reserve requirement	7% of total deposits	7% of total deposits, 7% of non-resident baht account and 7% of short-term foreign borrowings	1995-1996
		A reduction from 7% to 6% for total deposits	1997
5. Ownership of non-financial business	10% of a company's shares	Approval required if holding exceeds 10%	1994
6. Credits ratings		First credit rating agency The Thai Rating & Information Service (TRIS) started	1993
7. Stock market regulation		Securities and Exchange Commission founded. Public companies can issue corporate bonds & debentures to general public	1992

Source: Intarachote and Williams, 2003

Note: 1/ Banks are advised to base their lending on the Minimum Lending Rate (MLR), Minimum Overdraft Rate (MOR) and Minimum Retail Rate (MRR). A maximum margin must be added to the MRR as a reference rate for customers other than those eligible for MLR.

3.3. Literature Review

There are three strands of literature which relate to the present study: (1) those relating to bank efficiency which includes the methodologies of measuring bank efficiency, (2) those dealing with the impact of international financial integration on bank efficiency and (3) those studying bank efficiency in Asia including Thailand.

3.3.1 Bank Efficiency

Berger and Hamphrey (1997) surveyed 130 studies of financial institution efficiency in 21 countries, covering various types of depository institutions including commercial banks, savings and loans, and credit unions – as well as insurance firms. The studies surveyed five different econometric techniques of measuring efficiency with the aim at summarising and critically reviewing empirical estimates of financial institutions efficiency. They focused on frontier efficiency, in other words, how close financial institutions are to a 'best-practice' frontier. Frontier analysis is a complicated way to benchmark the relative performance of production units. Generally, studies of frontier efficiency are based on accounting measures of costs, outputs, inputs, revenues, profits etc. to calculate efficiency relative to the best practice within the available sample because engineering information on the technology of financial institutions is not available. The five major different econometric techniques for estimating efficiency frontiers are *nonparametric frontiers*[7] which include, for example, (1) data envelopment analysis (DEA), (2) free disposal hull (FDH), and *parametric frontiers*[8] which comprise three main approaches: (3) stochastic

---

[7] DEA is a linear programming technique where the set of best-practice or frontier observations is the one for which no other linear combination of units has as much or more of every output (given inputs) or as little or less of every input (given outputs). FDH is a special case of the DEA model where the points on lines connecting the DEA vertices are not included in the frontier (Beger and Hamphrey, p. 5, 1997).

[8] SFA specifies a functional form for the cost, profit, or production relationship among inputs, outputs, and environmental factors, and allows for random error. SFA suggests a composed error model where inefficiencies are assumed to follow an asymmetric distribution, normally the half-normal, whereas random errors follow a symmetric distribution, usually the standard normal. The inefficiencies must have a truncated distribution because inefficiencies cannot be negative. DFA specifies a functional form for the frontier but separate the inefficiencies from random in a different way. DFA assumes that the efficiency of each firm is stable over time whereas random error tends to average out to zero over time. Unlike SFA, DFA has no strong assumptions relating to the specific distributions of the inefficiencies or random errors. Based on DFA, inefficiencies can be almost of any form of distribution, even one that is relatively close to symmetric as long as the inefficiencies are nonnegative. The last approach is TFA. TFA specifies form and assumes that deviations from predicted performance values within the highest and lowest performance quartiles of observations classified by size class represent random error. At the same time, deviations in predicted performance between the highest and

frontier approach (SFA), (4) distribution-free approach (DFA) and (5) thick frontier approach (TFA). They found that the various efficiency methods do not always yield consistent results. Results from applications of efficiency analysis suggest that deregulation of financial institutions can either improve or worsen efficiency. It depends on industry conditions prior to deregulation[9].

Casu et al. (2004) compared parametric and non-parametric estimates of productivity changes in European banking between 1994 and 2000. Productivity change has been further decomposed into technological change, or change in best practice, and efficiency change. The findings suggest that productivity growth mainly came from improvements in technology and it seems unlikely that there was a catch-up on the part of non best-practice institutions. They also found that although competing methodologies sometimes identify conflicting findings for the sources of productivity growth for individual years, the two approaches do not yield significantly different results in terms of identifying the components of productivity growth during the 1990s. Mester (1996) used the stochastic cost frontier approach to examine bank efficiency in the Third Federal Reserve District taking into account the quality and risk of bank output. The findings suggest that Third District banks operated at cost-efficient output levels and product mixes. However, there appears to be a significant level of X-inefficiency at the banks. With reference of coping with increased competitive pressures, inefficient banks in the Third District have more to fear from banks that are efficient producers than from banks that are producers with particular output level or product mixes. There is less cost savings advantage from changing output size or mix than from using inputs more cost-effectively.

Berger et al. (2004) tested the effects of the relative health of community banks on economic growth. The analysis employed data between 1993 and 2000 on the economic performance and financial systems of 49 developed and developing countries. The study suggests that greater market shares and efficiency ranks of small, private, domestically owned banks facilitate better economic performance. The coefficients on the interaction terms between market shares and efficiency ranks are positive and statistically significant for both developed and developing countries indicating that the marginal benefits of higher shares for community banks are greater when these banks are more efficient. Mahajan et al. (1996) studied evidence on the economies of scale, subadditivity and efficiency in U.S. multinational and domestic banking. The results indicate that the cost structures of multinational banks and domestic

---

lowest quartiles represent inefficiencies and random error exists within these quartiles (Berger and Hamphrey, 1997).

[9] For example, in many countries, deregulation led to rapid branch expansion, excessive asset growth, bank failures, and reduced efficiency. In fact, one of the objectives of deregulation is to improve efficiency, nevertheless, other objectives may intervene (Beger and Hamphrey, 1997, p. 4).

banks are different. Multinational banks are able to fully utilise economies of scale and have lesser diseconomies from joint production and lower inefficiencies than domestic banks.

3.3.2 Impact of International Financial Integration on Bank Efficiency

With reference to the impact of financial liberalisation on performance of financial institutions, Fohlin (2000) studied the German universal banking system in the pre-WW I period in comparison with American and British banking systems with an objective of examining whether universality[10] affects banking industry concentration, the level of market power, or the financial performance of banks. The empirical results suggest that universality is not linked with superior profitability, whether the hypothesised source is efficiency (economies of scope) or monopoly power.

Claessens, Demirguc-Kunt and Huizinga (2001) found that foreign banks achieve higher profits than domestic banks in developing countries, while the reverse is not true in developed countries. The differences of financial conditions between foreign and domestic banks are attributed to differences in customer base, bank procedures, regulatory and tax regimes. Crystal et al. (2001) suggested that foreign ownership may provide important positive effects on the stability and development of emerging market banking systems. Majnoni et al. (2003) indicated that in the case of Hungary foreign banks are more successful in product innovation, offer a broader range of financial services and have better screening and monitoring procedures than domestic banks. Clarke et al. (2001) suggested that if foreign bank entry is broad enough to exert competitive pressure on domestic banks, this will benefit consumers. On the other hand, foreign banks could be a source of financial instabilities in developing countries if they decrease their exposures to those countries during crisis times. Claessens and Laeven (2003) found that greater foreign bank presence and fewer activity restrictions in the banking sector can lead to more competition in banking systems. Based on data for the post-deregulation in Australia during the period 1988-2001, Sturm and Williams (2004) found that foreign banks were more efficient than domestic banks but the higher efficiency did not imply higher foreign bank profit. Bank efficiency has significantly increased during the post-deregulation. Interestingly, diversity in the types of banks was found to be an important source of improvements in productivity. Detragiache and Gupta (2004) argued that even subsidiaries of foreign banks in

---

[10] Universality is the combination of commercial and investment banking services. Germany has been one of the first and most enthusiastic developers of large scale, joint-stock, mixed banks. In the decades leading up to WW I, the British financial system was the most specialised. On the other hand, at the start of the 20th century, the American banks were quasi-universal, because most significant investment houses maintained commercial bank affiliates, usually as subsidiaries (Fohlin, 2000).

Malaysia were not necessarily invulnerable to the financial crises which struck in many emerging countries in 1997.

As far as the link of foreign bank presence, domestic bank performance and financial development is concerned, there are both positive and negative impacts of foreign bank participation on the domestic banking industry and economy (Claessens, Demirguc-Kunt and Huizinga, 2000, 2001, Mishkin 2000, Goldberg, Dages and Kinney, 2000, and Sabi, 1996). For example, foreign banks in Hungary are more profitable than domestic banks and did not expose themselves to a greater liquidity or credit risk. They provided less consumer loans and were reluctant to give long-term loans (Sabi, 1996). More multinational bank entry caused a lower total credit supply in the Polish economy during the early transition phase, which led to adverse effects on business investment (Weller, 1999).

3.3.3 Asian Studies on Bank Efficiency

Kwan (2003) examined the banking industry's per unit operating costs in seven Asian economies, comprising Hong Kong, Indonesia, Malaysia, Philippines, Singapore, South Korea and Thailand. The study is based on commercial banks which are listed in the IBCA bank credit rating agencies Bankscope database[11] between 1992 and 1999. The study shows that the country ranking of per unit labour costs and the country ranking of per unit physical capital costs are highly related. Banks with high labour costs also faced high capital cost. There are systematic differences in bank operating efficiency across these Asian countries; however, bank operating efficiency seems to be unrelated to the degree of openness of the banking sector. The study also finds that bank operating costs among these Asian countries declined between 1992 and 1997, suggesting that on average banks improved their operating performance over time. In 1997, the banks increased per unit operating costs when they dealt with their problem loans while output decreased. Between 1997 and 1999, the labour cost shares of the banks significantly declined but physical capital input was less flexible. Importantly, significant differences in the labour cost share are found across countries indicating that different countries have different bank production functions.

Mori and Tsutsui (1993) investigated the industrial organisational features of the financial markets in Thailand and their role in economic development and examined whether or not the market-structure-performance hypothesis is valid by estimating profit and cost functions. The study is based on pooled data from

[11] Bankscope does not include foreign branches and agencies that are wholly owned by foreign banks. Consequently, most of the sample banks are locally owned. However, the ownership status somehow does not clear-cut because it is possible for foreigners to own stocks of local banks (Kwan, 2003, p. 474).

1983-1987 of the commercial banks, finance companies, the securities companies and the mortgage credit companies which constituted the main part of the private financial intermediaries in Thailand. The findings are as follows: the expense rate of the commercial banks between 1983 and 1987 in Thailand was considerably higher than that of Japanese banks; however, their profit rate was not much higher and the real cost of funds was not so different. The market concentration in Thailand was higher than that in Japan. Economies of scale for both commercial banks and other financial institutions in Thailand were not found. For the commercial banks in Thailand, the effect of higher concentration on profits was positive. The oligopoly market structure of the commercial banks seemed to cause wasteful expenditure of banks. The policy implication from the findings is that it seems desirable to encourage new entry and limit the size of large banks in order to reduce their market power.

Leightner and Lovell (1998) constructed Malmquist growth indexes and productivity indexes for two different specifications of banks' objectives: commercial banks objective (profit–orientation, i.e. maximizing net interest income and non-interest income) and Bank of Thailand's objective (fostering economic growth by maximising credits granted and investments in securities) during 1989-1994. The findings are as follows: 1) under the right conditions, financial liberalisation can contribute to growth in banks' ability to increase their profits and in their ability to finance economic growth. 2) With reference to BOT objectives, the average bank experienced rapid growth relative to the previous year's best practice; however, the average Thai bank experienced falling total factor productivity growth (TFP) while the average foreign bank experienced raising TFP. 3) No matter what performance index is used or whether commercial bank or BOT objectives are used, the performance of foreign small banks improved more than other bank categories. Importantly, strong growth should not be always accepted as good. In contrast, regulators should keep careful watch in order to prevent rapid growth based on speculation.

Menkhoff (2000) studied bad banking in Thailand with an empirical analysis of macro indicators, revealing that long-term performance of Thailand's financial system is reasonable compared to other countries' experience. Nevertheless, the rapid liberalisation process resulted in severe problems of financial institutions; for example, it increased new kinds of credit risk and market risk. Consequently, formerly good banking practices became inadequate banking. Menkhoff and Suwanaporn (2003) analysed 560 credit files in the pre-crisis period (1992-1996) from Thai commercial banks. The study reveals that the structure in lending determinants is similar to those found in mature markets. The rationale of Thai commercial banks' lending was reasonable, and does not comply easily with the frequent belief that these banks played a major role in the crisis in the late 1990s.

With reference to the impact of foreign bank entry on the domestic banking sector, Herberholz (2002) found that foreign bank entry led to greater efficiency in the Thai domestic commercial banking sector. The narrowing of net interest margins suggests greater competition which provided welfare gains for both depositors and borrowers. The concomitant decline in profitability of domestic banks illustrates a decrease in excessive profits arising from oligopoly markets. However, an increase in cost margins (overhead expenses over total assets) seems to reflect financial restructuring efforts due to pressure from foreign bank entry. Interestingly, unlike what was found for other developing countries, foreign bank entry through the acquisition of locally incorporated banks had a stronger effect on the efficiency of the domestic commercial banking system in Thailand than had entry through the establishment of branches Herberholz (2002). Based on qualitative information, Intarachote and Williams (2003) found that foreign banks introduced due diligence and the monitoring, evaluating and disclosing of credit risks. This implies that foreign banks use their superior management skills and culture, while domestic banks base their improvement on a learning-by-doing process.

Overall, what we learned from the previous work can be grouped into four main points. Firstly, the various different econometric techniques for estimating efficiency frontiers do not always yield consistent results. Secondly, inefficient banks seem to have more fear from banks that are efficient producers than from banks that are producers with particular scale efficiency or scope efficiency. There is less cost saving advantage from changing output level or mix than from using inputs more cost-effectively. Thirdly, there are both positive and negative effects of foreign bank participation on the domestic banking industry and economy. Deregulation of financial institutions which can either improve or worsen efficiency depends on industry conditions prior to deregulation. Diversity in types of banks is likely to be an important source of improvements in productivity. Fourthly, the hasty liberalisation process without logical sequence resulted in severe problems of financial institutions. Formerly good banking practices become inadequate banking in consequence of new kinds of credit and market risks

3.4. Data and Methodology

3.4.1 Data and Descriptive Analysis

3.4.1.1 Data

The use of panel data provides many benefits for econometric estimation, for example, in three areas: 1) identification of economic models and discriminating between competing economic hypotheses, 2) eliminating and decreasing estimation bias, and 3) reducing problems of data multi-collinearity[12]. On the other hand, the special features of panel data can also create new and difficult econometric problems, in particular in nonlinear models (Hsiao, 1986).

This study includes two types of data. The first data set which is used for the descriptive analysis is at an aggregate level of balance sheets between 1988 and 2003 and income statements between 1992 and 2003 of domestic and foreign banks. It comes from the databank of financial institutions compiled by the Data Management Department, Bank of Thailand. According to the Commerical Banking act Act B.E. 1962 (No.2) and its amendments, a local bank and a branch of a foreign bank which receive licences can undertake the business of commercial banking. Unlike local banks, branches of foreign banks mostly concentrate on large multinational corporation clients. The second data set is bank level panel data of income statements and balance sheets of domestic and foreign banks in Thailand covering 9 years between 1995 and 2003 for the regression analysis. The bank level panel data set covers 23 out of a total of 31 commercial banks as of December 2003 which accounted for almost 90 percent of total assets of banking systems. It excludes Japanese banks and some foreign banks which possess differences in the start and end of the accounting year. The banks can be classified into three groups; nine domestic banks (representing both local private and state-owned banks), four joint venture banks (representing banks with more than 50 per cent of foreign ownership since the acquisitions by foreign banks in 1999[13]) and ten full branches of foreign banks (representing banks with 100 per cent of foreign ownership). The bank level panel data are based on financial data from the Stock Exchange of Thailand and bank annual reports.

---

[12] Baltagi (1995) stated that there are several benefits from using panel data. These include the following: (1) Panel data suggest that individuals, firms, states or countries are heterogeneous. (2) Panel data gives more informative data, more variability, less collinearity among the variables, more degrees of freedom and more efficiency. (3) Panel data are better to study the dynamics of adjustment. (4) Panel data are better to measure effects that cannot simply capture in pure cross-sections or pure time-series data. (5) Panel data models allow us to construct and test more complicated behavioural models than purely cross-section or time-series data. (6) Panel data are normally gathered on micro units, like individuals, firms and households and many variables can be more accurately measured at the micro level. However, there still are some limitations of panel data which include design and data collection problem, distortions of measurement errors, selectivity problems and short time-series dimension.

[13] On June 27, 1997 the Government issued an Emergency Decree amending the Commercial Banking Act B.E. 2505 (1962) (No. 2), amended in 1979 and 1992 (BOT, 2001). The Emergency Decree relaxed existing restrictions on the foreign ownership of commercial banks by allowing 100% shareholding for foreign investors who step in to resolve or rehabilitate financial institutions, subject to certain conditions. In fact, foreign investors are permitted to acquire a majority ownership interest in locally-incorporated financial institutions for a period of 10 years when new foreign equity will be limited to 49 percent.

3.4.1.2 Descriptive Analysis from Aggregated Data

Figure 3.1 illustrate main financial ratios relating market share and profitability of domestic banks[14] and foreign banks which were calculated from aggregated data (see table 3.A.1). Although domestic banks still held a large market share during the post-crisis period, foreign banks had gradually increased their market share, particularly in term of equity. As for profitability, ROA (after-tax income to total asset) of domestic banks experienced a net loss during 1997-2000 and turned to a profit during 2001-2003. On the other hand, although foreign banks experienced a decline in ROA during the post-crisis year, averaged ROA of foreign banks recorded positive figures both in the pre-crisis and post-crisis periods. The ratio of interest income to total assets of domestic banks was higher than that of foreign banks in the pre-crisis period, but lower in the post-crisis years. The market share in term of equity of foreign banks has

Figure 3.1: Market Shares and Profitability of Domestic and Foreign banks, 1992-2003

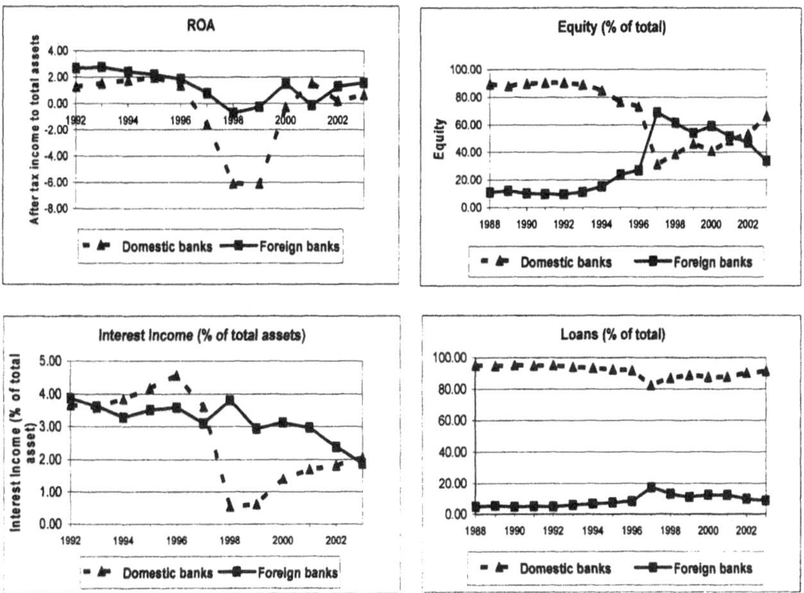

14 Domestic banks include four merged banks which have more than 50% of foreign ownership. Foreign banks participation is greater if taking into account of four merged banks after the crisis years and foreign investor's participation in large domestic banks when they increased their capital after the outbreak of the crisis.

Figures 3.2: Operating Costs and Loans of Domestic and Foreign banks, 1992- 2003

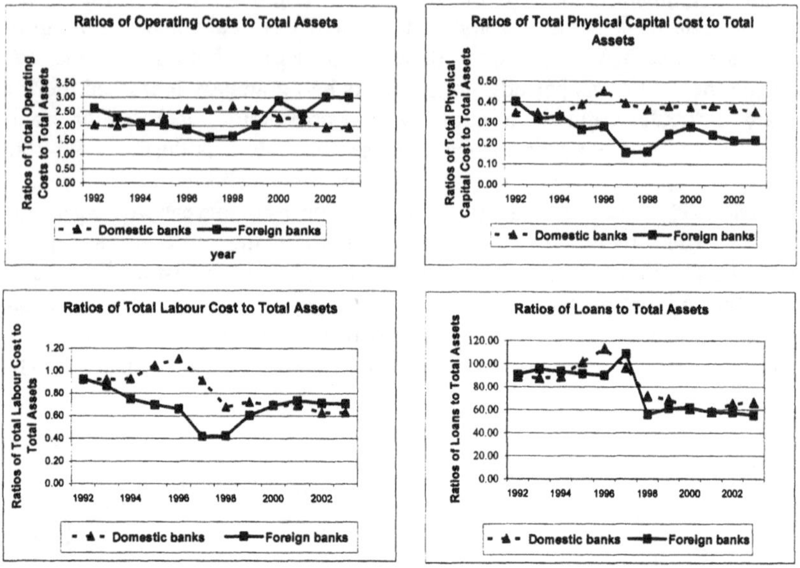

increased since the post-crisis years whereas the market share in term of loans of foreign banks have slightly changed.

According to figure 3.2, during the post-crisis period, domestic banks gradually decreased their operating costs to total assets whereas the operating costs to total assets of foreign banks slightly increased. The gap between labour cost to total assets of domestic and foreign banks became smaller during the post-crisis period. The physical capital costs to total assets of domestic banks were higher than that of foreign banks in most years both in the pre-crisis and post-crisis periods. The ratios of loans to total assets of both domestic and foreign banks moved in the same pattern. In fact, from table 3.A.2, the ratio of loans to total assets of domestic banks decreased from an average of 90.55 percent during 1988-1996 to an average 65.21 percent during 1998-2003. On the other hand, the loan to asset ratio of foreign banks declined from an average of 91.16 percent to an average of 58.18 percent during the same periods.

3.4.2 Methodology

In theory, if the objective of the firms is to maximise profits, the firms will choose the cost-minimising production plans for every level of output. This behaviour will be observed whether the firms are monopolists, perfect competitors or anything between, provided that they are perfectly competitive on their input markets and that therefore they face given input prices. There is a duality between production and cost, and as a result, we can use the cost function to generate a production function (Jehle and Reny, 2001). A production function is efficient when the maximum output is produced by each input level; in other words, the minimum level of each input is used for producing a given output (Maggi and Rossie, 2003).

Although there are a huge number of studies in bank efficiency, there does not seem to be a general agreement on how to define inputs and outputs of multi-product financial firms[15]. As a result, the choices made by researchers should be a pragmatic compromise between the theoretical point of view and data availability (Maggi and Rossie, 2003). However, it should be noted that different efficiency concepts suggest that each concept measures a different type of optimisation. At the same time, the choices concerning measurement technique, functional form, and other variables normally provide very little differences in either average industry efficiency or the ranking of individual firms in the data set (Berger and Mester, 1997).

In this paper, there are three sets of concerns: the first is to compare the banking production costs between different bank types in Thailand, the second is to explore the choice of input mix in bank cost function and the third is the effects of foreign bank entry on cost efficiency in the Thai banking industry. Similar to Kwan's paper (2003), total operating costs consist of labour costs, physical capital costs and other costs and exclude the funding cost component which is assumed to significantly depend on domestic interest rates. The per unit cost measure can be constructed in two ways; total operating cost to total assets according to the asset approach of the banking output concept, and total operating cost to the sum of total assets and total deposits in line with the intermediation approach.

3.4.2.1 Cost Efficiency

I employ the translog cost function specification which is similar to the methodology used by Kwan (2003). In fact, the translog cost function is one of the most used functional forms in the empirical studies on bank efficiency (Maggi and Rossie, 2003). Cost efficiency provides a measure of how close a bank's cost is to best practice for producing the same output bundle under the

---

[15] There are five most used approaches in the researches in this area. The first is the *production approach* which defines bank activities as production of services. The second is the *intermediate approach* which defines banks as financial intermediaries that purchase input in order to generate earning assets. The third is the *asset approach* which is a variant of the intermediation approach and defines liabilities as inputs and assets as output. The fourth is the *value added approach* which views any balance sheet item as output if it absorbs a relevant share of capital and labour. Otherwise it is treated as an input or non relevant output. The fifth is the *user cost approach* which states that the net contribution to the bank revenue that explains inputs and output (Maggi and Rossie, 2003).

same conditions. In other words, efficiency is defined relative to the best practice observed in the industry, rather than to any true minimum costs since the underlying technology is unknown (Berger and Mester, 1997 and Berger et al., 2004). The inefficiency which may cause costs higher than the best-practice level and random terms, u_c and ε_c, are assumed to be multiplicatively separated from the rest of the cost function as follows:

$$lnC = f(w, y, z, v) + ln u_C + ln \varepsilon_C \tag{1}$$

where f denotes a functional form. C measures variable costs, w is the vector of prices of variable inputs, y is the vector of quantities of variable outputs, z represents the quantities of any fixed netputs (inputs or outputs), v is a set of environmental or market variables which may affect performance, u_c shows an inefficiency factor which may raise costs higher than the best-practice level and ε_c presents the random error (Berger and Mester, 1997). In fact, the $ln u_c$ term is a factor that represents a bank's inefficiency and $ln \varepsilon_c$ is a random error which incorporates both measurement error and luck. The cost function is estimated using the ($ln u_c + ln \varepsilon_c$) as a composite error term (Berger et al., 2004).

In order to minimise the fundamental statistical problem arising from any omitted variables which are correlated with the included explanatory variables, one of three methods[16] when panel data are available is that of using dummy variables to capture the effects of time-invariant variables such as an individual-firm management and/or individual-invariant variables such as prices and interest rates. The pooled OLS estimate is generally consistent, although it is inefficient because it does not incorporate any prior knowledge about the form of serial correlation (Johnston and Dinardo, 1997). In contrast, the coefficients produced by the fixed-effects model (or also called least-squares dummy-variable approach) remain unbiased and consistent (Johnston and Dinardo, 1997, Hsiao, 1986). In response to these arguments, I tested both pooled OLS and fixed effects and between regressions. The paper presents the results from the pooled regressions which provide much power in explanation. I specify the widely used translog functional form to estimate whether production costs vary systematically across banks and over time:

<u>Panel A</u>: Domestic, Merged and Foreign Banks

$$\begin{aligned} lnC_{jt} = \alpha + \beta_1 lnX_{jt} + \beta_2 DOMESTIC * lnX_{jt} + \beta_3\ FOREIGN * lnX_{jt} + \gamma_1 FOREIGN \\ + \gamma_2 MERGED + \delta_1 DC_t + \delta_2 FOREIGN * DC_t + \delta_3 MERGED * DC_t + ln\varepsilon_{jt}. \end{aligned} \tag{2}$$

[16] The other two methods are as follows: 1) differencing the sample observations to reducing the individual-specific and/or time-specific effects and 2) assuming a conditional distribution of unobserved effects, given observed exogenous variables (Hsiao, 1986: p. 215-216).

Panel B: Domestic and Merged Banks (Foreign Bank Entry Effects on Cost Efficiency)

$$\ln C_{jt} = \alpha + \beta_1 \ln X_{jt} + \beta_2 MERGED * \ln X_{jt} + \gamma\, MERGED + \delta_1\, acquiredyr_t + \delta_2\, MERGED * acquiredyr_t + \ln \varepsilon_{jt} \qquad (3)$$

It is should be noted that dummy variables for the ownership and time effect capture ln_{u_c}.

$\ln C_{jt}$ is the natural logarithm of the dependent variable of observed cost over total assets for the *j*th bank at year *t*; three separate equations are estimated with total operating costs, labour costs and physical capital costs as dependent variables, respectively.

$\ln X_{jt}$ is the vector of the natural logarithm of the independent variables; it includes cash and inter-bank/total assets, loan loss provisions/total loans[17], equity capital /total assets, loans/total assets and other earning assets[18]/total assets.

DOMESTIC is a dummy which takes on the value 1 if the banks are domestic banks and 0 otherwise, *MERGED* is 1 if the banks are merged banks and 0 otherwise and *FOREIGN* is 1 if the banks are foreign banks and 0 otherwise. *DOMESTIC* is excluded as the reference category.

*DOMESTIC**independent variables and *FOREIGN**independent variables are the interaction terms between domestic and foreign banks and independent variables respectively. The interaction terms allow for different slope coefficients across different types of banks or in other words, they allow for bank-specific characteristics such as bank management styles.

DC is a time specific dummy variable for the financial crisis (*DC* =1 if period >= 1998 and *DC* = 0 if period <= 1997). I also tested for regressions which include yearly dummy variables; however, most of those coefficients were insignificant.

*FOREIGN*DC* and *MERGED*DC* are the interaction terms between foreign banks and post-crisis periods and merged banks and post-crisis periods, respectively.

acquiredyr is a time specific dummy variable for the period of foreign bank entry through acquisitions after the crisis (acquiredyr=1 if period >= 2000 and acquiredyr = 0 if period <= 1999). Four local private banks were completely acquired by foreign banks in 1999.

---

[17] As for X_2 loan loss provisions/total loans, I use the ratio figure of loan loss provisions/total net loans rather than natural log of that ratio in order to avoid of losing some observations because some observations are zero and negative figures. Total loans are defined as net loans which are loans less allowance for possible loan loss.

[18] The other earning assets include securities purchased under resale agreements and investments in securities.

*MERGED**acquiredyr is the interaction term between merged banks and the foreign bank acquisition year.

α ,β , γ and δ are the vectors of regression coefficients; and ε_{it} is the error term.

Followed Kwan (2003), the ratio of cash and inter-bank assets to total assets (x_1) captures *the liquidity of banks*. Although liquid assets reduce the bank's liquidity risk, they seem more costly to manage since these assets involve additional transportation cost, storage and protection costs and labour cost. Consequently, the coefficient of the cash ratio is expected to be positive. The ratio of loan loss provision to total loans (x_2) controls for *output quality*. The coefficient of the ratio of loan loss provisions can be either negative or positive. If banks spend more of their resources on credit underwriting and loan monitoring, they would have less loan loss provisions. Then, the coefficient would be negative. However, if loan quality is endogenous in the quality management, an efficient bank with low operating costs would have less problem loans and consequently, less loans loss provisions. Thus, the coefficient would be positive. The ratio of equity capital to total assets (x_3) represents the *quality of bank management and risk preference*. Banks which have high equity capital, indicating both high quality management and aversion to risk taking, are more likely to have higher cost efficiency. As a result, the coefficient on the equity ratio is expected to be negative. The loans to total assets (x_4) capture the *output mix*. Because loans seem to be more costly to produce than investment securities, the coefficient of loans to total assets is assumed to be positive (Kwan, 2003). One difference from Kwan's work (2003) is that I propose the other earning assets to total assets (x_5) to control for output mix. Similar to the loan to total assets, the coefficient of the other earning assets to total assets is anticipated to be positive.

There are two types of dummy variables; one is the dummy variables for the ownership and the second is the time specific dummy variables. The dummy variables for the ownership capture whether there are systematic differences in operating costs across different types of ownerships (domestic, merged and foreign banks). The coefficients of the dummy variables for the ownership capture bank specific factors which include the productivity of labour, the efficiency in resource utilisation and management styles. The dummy variable for domestic banks is excluded and defined as a reference category[19]. The time

[19] One of the bank specific dummy variables is excluded and defined as a reference category so as to be assured of the existence of the inverse of $(X'X)^{-1}$ matrix which is important in OLS because it is necessary for computing the estimator $\hat{\beta}$. The determinant $(X'X)$ > 0 which means no multicollinearity between the explanatory variables (multicollinearity relates to the event that two or more explanatory variables are strongly linearly correlated). In fact, X_i is

specific dummy variables control whether there are systematic changes in production costs over time, particularly pre- and post-crisis.

3.4.2.2 Choice of Input

The second set of concerns is to investigate whether the choice of input-mix, for example, the mix of labour and physical capital varies systematically across banks and over time:

Panel A: Domestic, Merged and Foreign Banks

$$\ln M_{jt} = \alpha + \beta_1 \ln X_{jt} + \beta_2 DOMESTIC * \ln X_{jt} + \beta_3 FOREIGN * \ln X_{jt} + \gamma_1 FOREIGN + \gamma_2 MERGED + \delta_1 DC_t + \delta_2 FOREIGN * DC_t + \delta_3 MERGED * DC_t + \ln \varepsilon_{jt} \quad (4)$$

Panel B: Domestic and Merged Banks (Foreign Bank Entry Effects on Choice of Input)

$$\ln M_{jt} = \alpha + \beta_1 \ln X_{jt} + \beta_2 MERGED * \ln X_{jt} + \gamma MERGED + \delta_1 acquiredyr_t + \delta_2 MERGED * acquiredyr_t + \ln \varepsilon_{jt} \quad (5)$$

where $\ln M_{jt}$ is the natural logarithm of the dependent variable of observed cost for the jth bank at year t; (M_1 = labour cost to total operating costs, M_2= physical capital cost/total operating costs). Other variables of the right hand side of the equations 4 and 5 are the same as explained for equations 2 and 3.

3.5. Empirical Results

3.5.1 Cost efficiency

Based on equation 2, table 3.2 reports the cost efficiency of domestic and foreign banks in terms of total operating costs. The t-statistics are computed by using heteroscedasticity-corrected robust standard errors. There are two regressions; regression 1 presents the ratio of total operating costs/total assets and regression 2 presents the ratio of total operating costs /total assets plus deposits. Similar to Kwan's paper (2003), the results from regression 1 and 2 render almost the same results. Most of the coefficients have the same sign as expected from the theory. Taking the bank-specific characteristics such as bank management style into account by allowing for the different slope coefficients across types of banks, the results from regression 1 and 2 suggest that the operating costs of domestic banks are significantly positively related to cash and inter-bank assets, loan loss provisions and other earning assets but unrelated to equity and loans. On the other hands, those of foreign banks are significantly negatively related to equity and positively related to other earning assets but unrelated to cash and inter-bank assets, loan loss provisions, and loans. The

---

not allowed to be an exact function of all other explanatory variables. If det $(X'X) = 0$ (has multicollinearity), the inverse of $(X'X)$ is not defined. As a result, we cannot calculate the least squares estimator $\hat{\beta}$ (Christensen, 2001).

Table 3.2: Regression Results (Panel A): The Comparison of Cost Efficiency of Domestic and Foreign Banks: Total Operating Costs

Independent Variables	Dependent Variables:OPERATING COSTS	
	Regression 1 Operating costs/total assets	**Regression 2** Operating costs/total assets+deposits
	parameter t-stat	**parameter t-stat**
Cash and Interbank/Total Assets	-0.0238 (-0.21)	-0.0382 (-0.35)
Loan Loss Provisions/Total Loans	**-0.5635*** (2.94)**	**-0.5620*** (3.21)**
Equity/Total Assets	0.1675 (1.09)	0.2071 (1.42)
Loans/Total Assets	**0.3634** (2.12)**	**0.3812** (2.27)**
Other Earning Assets/Total Assets	**-0.2809** (-2.12)**	**-0.3216** (2.42)**
*DOMESTIC** Cash and Interbank/Total Assets	**0.2803** (2.16)**	**0.2754** (2.16)**
*DOMESTIC** Loan Loss Provisions/Total Loans	**2.8661** (2.07)**	**3.1870** (2.37)**
*DOMESTIC** Equity/Total Assets	-0.2528 (-1.44)	**-0.2976* (-1.75)**
*DOMESTIC** Loans/Total Assets	0.3849 (1.55)	0.2826 (1.08)
*DOMESTIC** Other Earning Assets/Total Assets	**0.4182*** (2.86)**	**0.4445*** (3.00)**
*FOREIGN** Cash and Interbank/Total Assets	0.1515 (1.18)	0.1510 (1.22)
*FOREIGN** Loan Loss Provisions/Total Loans	1.0818 (1.48)	1.0436 (1.39)
*FOREIGN** Equity/Total Assets	**-0.4938*** (-3.02)**	**-0.4589*** (-2.95)**
*FOREIGN** Loans/Total Assets	-0.1585 (-0.76)	-0.1724 (-0.85)
*FOREIGN** Other Earning Assets/Total Assets	**0.4941*** (3.31)**	**0.4985*** (3.36)**
FOREIGN	-0.3348 (-0.77)	0.1472 (0.33)
MERGED	**-1.2741* (-1.89)**	**-1.1641* (-1.74)**
DC	-0.0707 (0.82)	-0.1202 (-1.34)
FOREIGN *DC	0.1124 (0.86)	0.1207 (0.91)
MERGED *DC	**0.6986*** (5.08)**	**0.7248*** (5.42)**
Intercept	**-2.9029*** (-8.79)**	**-3.5850*** (-10.51)**
R-squared	0.4419	0.5523
Number of Obs.	200	200
Number of Banks	23	23

Notes:
1) DOMESTIC*independent variables and FOREIGN*independent variables are the interaction between domestic and foreign banks and independent variables respectively.
2) FOREIGN*DC and MERGED*DC are the interaction terms between foreign banks and post-crisis period and merged banks and post-crisis periods respectively.
3) The regressions are estimated by using ordinary least squared pooled cross-bank time-series data.
4) * denotes 10% level of significance, ** denotes 5% level of significance, and *** denotes 1% level of significance and t-statistics which are reported in the parentheses are calculated by using heteroscedasticity-corrected robust standard errors.

findings illustrate that the production costs of domestic and foreign banks are different resulting from differences in business structures, management styles and customer bases (also see Claessens et. al., 2001).

In fact, domestic banks concentrated on reducing liquidity risk by holding high levels of cash and inter-bank which led to high operating costs. Domestic banks also had high levels of non-performing loans (the ratio of loan loss provisions to total loans). In contrast, foreign banks were well-capitalised banks and more focused on the quality of bank management and risk aversion (the ratio of equity capital to total assets). The results highlight that foreign banks seemed to have better quality of bank management and risk preference and lower levels of non-performing loans, compared to domestic banks. This finding is consistent with Detragiache and Gupta (2004)'s study which indicates that foreign banks in Malaysia had relatively low non-performing loans; at the same time, their profitability and capitalisation improved during the crisis. In contrast, domestic banks in Malaysia had experienced rapid portfolio growth before the crisis and most of them concentrated in the property sector and the share purchase sector which experienced strong losses.

Domestic banks concentrated on holding high levels of liquid assets, whereas foreign banks could receive liquidity and cash and other liquid assets from their headquarters. Interestingly, domestic and foreign banks had one thing in common. Their operating costs were significantly positively related to other earning assets, suggesting that banks engaged more in other earning assets which include securities purchased under resale agreements and investments in securities rather than concentrating in loans only. The reason for this is that after the 1997 financial crisis, banks faced a large amount of non performing loans, and as a result, banks moved towards other sources of earnings.

The coefficients on the interaction terms of other earning assets with the ownership dummies show by how much the marginal effect of other earning assets on costs differs across ownership categories. From regression 2, these coefficients are significantly positive and the marginal effect of other earning assets on costs is slightly stronger for foreign than for domestic banks. To obtain the overall marginal effect of other earning assets on costs for domestic banks, one has to add the coefficients on other earning assets (β_1) and on the interaction term (β_2). The result is 0.1229 (0.4445-0.3216). For foreign banks, the effect is even bigger at 0.1769 (0.4985-0.3216).

Table 3.3: Regression Results (Panel A): The Comparison of Cost Efficiency of Domestic and Foreign Banks: Labour and Physical Capital Costs

Independent Variables	Dependent Variables:LABOUR COST		Dependent Variables:CAPITAL COST	
	Regression 3 Labour cost/total assets **parameter t-stat**	**Regression 4** Labour cost/total assets+deposits **parameter t-stat**	**Regression 5** Capital cost/total assets **parameter t-stat**	**Regression 6** Capital cost/total assets+deposits **parameter t-stat**
Cash and Interbank/Total A.	0.0209 (0.14)	0.0065 (0.04)	-0.0962 (-0.94)	-0.1107 (-1.13)
Loan Loss Provisions/Total Loans	-0.1188 (-0.30)	-0.1174 (0.32)	**-0.4474*** (-3.36)**	**-0.4460*** (-3.36)**
Equity/ Total Assets	0.0264 (0.14)	0.0659 (0.36)	0.0213 (0.17)	0.0609 (0.49)
Loans/ Total Assets	0.2357 (1.06)	0.2535 (1.17)	0.0172 (0.14)	0.0350 (0.29)
Other Earning A./ Total A.	-0.1857 (-1.22)	-0.2264 (-1.58)	**-0.2171* (-1.93)**	**-0.2578** (-2.31)**
*DOMESTIC**Cash and Interbank/Total Assets	0.2343 (1.42)	0.2293 (1.45)	**0.2370* (1.95)**	**0.2321** (1.99)**
*DOMESTIC**Loan Loss Provisions/Total Loans	0.9747 (1.05)	1.2955 (1.46)	**1.7091*** (2.67)**	**2.0299*** (3.30)**
*DOMESTIC**Equity/Total Assets	-0.0750 (-0.37)	-0.1199 (-0.63)	-0.0640 (-0.47)	-0.1088 (-0.82)
*DOMESTIC**Loans/Total Assets	**0.5766** (2.19)**	**0.4743* (1.85)**	**0.7096*** (3.47)**	**0.6073*** (3.28)**
*DOMESTIC**Other Earning Assets/Total Assets	**0.3328** (2.08)**	**0.3590** (2.37)**	**0.3875*** (2.94)**	**0.4138*** (3.20)**
*FOREIGN**Cash and Interbank/Total Assets	0.1652 (1.01)	0.1647 (1.06)	**0.2467* (1.95)**	**0.2462** (2.03)**
*FOREIGN**Loan Loss Provisions/Total Loans	0.2570 (0.46)	0.2188 (0.42)	0.6587 (1.00)	0.6205 (0.99)
*FOREIGN**Equity/Total Assets	-0.2109 (-1.05)	-0.1761 (-0.93)	-0.1580 (-1.01)	-0.1232 (-0.81)
*FOREIGN**Loans/Total Assets	-0.1794 (-0.73)	-0.1933 (-0.82)	0.2551 (1.32)	0.2412 (1.30)
*FOREIGN**Other Earning Assets/Total Assets	**0.3320** (1.96)**	**0.3364** (2.15)**	**0.5251*** (3.55)**	**0.5295*** (3.71)**
FOREIGN	**-0.6074* (-1.69)**	-0.1255 (-0.37)	-0.0831 (-0.15)	0.3988 (0.77)
MERGED	**-1.4654* (-1.65)**	-1.3554 (-1.60)	**-1.6529*** (-2.85)**	**-1.5428*** (-2.75)**
DC	**-0.4005*** (-5.95)**	**-0.4500*** (-6.84)**	-0.1105 (-1.26)	**-0.1600* (-1.80)**
*FOREIGN**DC	**0.4009*** (3.34)**	**0.4091*** (3.59)**	-0.0171 (-0.10)	-0.0089 (-0.05)
*MERGED**DC	**0.6618*** (3.40)**	**0.6880*** (3.76)**	**0.6218*** (4.57)**	**0.6480*** (4.91)**
Intercept	**-3.6244*** (-15.72)**	**-4.3066*** (-19.06)**	**-4.7168*** (-12.41)**	**-5.3990*** (-15.17)**
R-squared	0.4441	0.6175	0.3212	0.2394
Number of Obs.	200	200	200	200
Number of Banks (Number of groups)	23	23	23	23

Notes:

1) DOMESTIC Dependent variables and FOREIGN*Dependent variables are the interaction between domestic and foreign banks and independent variables respectively.

2) FOREIGN*DC and MERGED*DC are the interaction terms between foreign banks and post-crisis period and merged banks and post-crisis periods respectively.

3) The regressions are estimated by using ordinary least squared pooled cross-bank time-series data.

4) * denotes 10% level of significance, ** denotes 5% level of significance, and *** denotes 1% level of significance and t-statistics which are reported in the parentheses are calculated by using heteroscedasticity-corrected robust standard errors.

The dummy variables for the ownership capture whether there are systematic differences in operating costs across banks. Unexpectedly, based on the estimated coefficients of dummy variables for the ownership, the unit costs of production of domestic and foreign banks are indistinguishable. In terms of bank operating efficiency, foreign banks did not outperform domestic banks. The findings suggest that if foreign banks represent the best-practice banks in the industry, to a large extent, domestic banks in Thailand have managed to catch up to the best-practice standard.

Regarding the time effect dummy variables, the coefficients of *DC* (crisis year dummy variable) and interaction term of *FOREIGN**DC* are insignificant, showing that per unit of production costs of both domestic and foreign banks during the post-crisis period are not significantly different. On the other hand, the coefficient of the interaction term *MERGED**DC* is significantly positive, illustrating that per unit of production costs of merged banks during the post-crisis period are higher than those of domestic and foreign banks. Possible reasons for the increase in operating costs of merged banks include the additional resources to operate with the massive non-performing loans at a time when the output deteriorated as well as, the financial restructuring in order to increase their competitiveness.

In order to illuminate the production process, table 3.3 presents the cost efficiency of domestic and foreign banks in terms of labour costs (regressions 3 and 4) and physical capital costs (regressions 5 and 6). Similar to regressions 1 and 2, the results from regressions 3 and 4 and regressions 5 and 6 give the similar results. Regressions 3 and 4 show that per unit labour costs of domestic banks are statistically positively related to loans and other earning assets and those of foreign banks are significantly positively related to other earning assets only, illustrating that loans and other earning assets are labour intensive. As for the domestic banks, the estimated coefficient of the interaction term of *DOMESTIC*loans* is higher than that of *DOMESTIC*other earning assets* (the calculation method is illustrated earlier), suggesting that loans are more costly to produce than investment securities, a finding which confirms with Kwan's (2003). Surprisingly, the marginal effects of interaction terms of *DOMESTIC*other earning assets* and *FOREIGN*other earning assets* are similar. One possible conclusion that can be drawn from this is that there are few differences between the marginal labour costs with respect to other earning assets of domestic and foreign banks.

In regression 4 (higher r-square), the estimated coefficients of dummy variables for ownership are insignificant, indicating that on average the labour productivity of domestic, merged and foreign banks is indistinguishable. The coefficient of the post-crisis years is significantly negative (-0.4500). The estimated coefficients of the interaction terms of both *FOREIGN*DC* and *MERGED*DC* are significantly negative and positive; -0.4500+0.4091= -0.0409 and -0.4500+0.6880 = +0.2380, respectively. The results suggest that after the crisis, per unit labour costs of domestic banks were lower than those of foreign banks. On the other hand, per unit labour costs of merged banks were higher than those of domestic banks. One reason is that merged banks had major downsizing and reorganisation in the early phase of acquisitions which incurred high costs, in particular the early retirement schemes. At the same time, after reorganisation, merged banks, like other foreign banks hired more high skilled labour with higher pay, compared with that of domestic banks. The evidence indicates that labour productivity in the banking sector in Thailand improved after the crisis, as it did in other Asian countries between 1992 and 1997 as found by Kwan (2003). The improvement of cost efficiency in the banking sector in term of labour productivity resulted from the financial restructuring which was forced upon banks by the crisis, by increased competition through the acquisitions of majority stakes in locally incorporated banks by foreign banks, by new technology and financial innovation and at the same time, was speeded up during the recent IMF rescue package.

The physical capital cost regressions (regressions 5 and 6) render generally similar results as the total operating cost regressions (regressions 1 and 2). In contrast, Kwan (2003) found that the labour cost regressions provide generally similar results to the total cost regressions. From regression 5 with higher r-square than regression 6), per unit physical capital costs of domestic banks are statistically positively related to cash and inter-bank assets, loan loss provisions, loans and other earning assets whereas those of foreign banks are significantly positively related to only cash and inter-bank assets and other earning assets. The coefficients on the interaction terms of other earning assets with the ownership dummies are positively significant. Surprisingly, the marginal effect of other earning assets on physical capital costs of foreign banks (0.3080: 0.5251-0.2171) is stronger than that of domestic banks (0.1704: 0.3875-0.2171), indicating that foreign banks utilised more physical capital in managing resale agreements and investments securities than domestic banks. As expected, the marginal effects of loans on physical capital costs of foreign banks (0.2723: 0.2551+0.0172) is lower than those of domestic banks (0.7268: 0.7096+0.0172), suggesting that foreign banks are more efficient in managing loans than domestic banks, which may result from either better monitoring systems and risk managements or better loan quality.

From regression 5, the estimated coefficient for merged banks is statistically negative; illustrating that per unit physical capital costs of merged banks were lower than those of domestic banks. On the other hand, per unit physical capital costs of domestic and foreign banks are indistinguishable. The coefficient of the post-crisis dummy is insignificant. At the same time, the estimated coefficient of the interaction term of *MERGED*DC* is significantly positive (0.5113: 0.6218-0.1105), suggesting that per unit capital costs of merged banks were higher than those of domestic and foreign banks. After the 1997 financial crisis, most banks embarked on restructuring processes which needed long term investment in physical resources. One explanation is that some banks introduced outsourcing for capital-intensive activities related to information technology, for example, information system engineering, IT infrastructure, and information system processing[20] (Manager Magazine, 2003). Another explanation is that an increase in advanced technology in banking services resulted in banks moving away from the 'bricks and mortar' concept of branch-based retail banking towards e-banking as pointed out by Herberholz (2002).

3.5.2 Choice of Input

It is generally accepted that there is substitution between labour and capital in the production process in the banking industry. This section tests whether the shares of labour and physical capital costs vary with the cash and inter-bank assets to total assets (the liquidity of the banks), the loan loss provision to total loans (output quality), the equity capital to total assets (quality of bank management and risk preference), loans to total assets and the other earning assets to total assets (output mix). The dummy variables for the ownership test whether there are systematic differences in labour and physical capital cost shares across different types of banks. The explanation of the variations among banks arises from remuneration and technology embracement across banks. The time specific dummy variables test for systematic time effects on labour and physical capital shares.

The results from regression 7 from table 3.4 estimated from equation 4 shows that the labour cost share of domestic banks is significantly negatively related to loan loss provisions whereas that of foreign banks is significantly positively related to equity. The result confirms the earlier finding in section 3.5.1 that production costs of domestic and foreign banks are different. One possible interpretation is that domestic and foreign banks have different businesses structures. Another possible interpretation is that domestic banks used more resources in handling non-performing loans; in contrast, foreign banks were well-capitalised banks and were more focused on the quality of bank management and prudent risk management. The estimated coefficients of the dummy variables for the ownership are insignificant, indicating that there are no significant differences among the three bank groups in terms of labour cost shares. Regarding the time effect dummy variables, the coefficient of the post-

---

[20] DBS Thai Dhanu bank which was acquired by DBS, Singapore in 1999 and has more than 50% of foreign ownership, firstly introduced outsourcing. At end-2002, Kasikorn Bank (formerly named Thai Farmer Bank) made the biggest outsourcing deal in Thailand with IBM, in the amount of 10,000 million baht for 10 years (Manager Magazine, 2003).

crisis dummy is significant negative. The estimated coefficient of the interaction term of *FOREIGN*DC* is significantly negative (-0.0413: 0.2885-0.3298), illustrating that the labour cost shares of domestic and foreign banks declined during the post-crisis period.

Table 3.4: Regression Results (Panel A) of the Labour and Physical Capital Cost Shares of Domestic and Foreign Banks

Independent Variables	**Dependent Variables: Labour and Capital Cost Shares**	
	Regression 7 Labour cost/total operating costs	**Regression 8** Capital cost/total operating cost
	parameter t-stat	parameter t-stat
Cash and Interbank/Total Assets	0.0447 (0.43)	-0.0724 (-1.48)
Loan Loss Provisions/Total Loans	**0.4446* (1.69)**	0.1160 (0.80)
Equity/Total Assets	-0.1411 (-1.08)	-0.1462 (-1.45)
Loans/Total Assets	-0.1277 (-0.89)	**-0.3462*** (-3.36)**
Other Earning Assets/Total Assets	0.0952 (0.73)	0.0638 (0.95)
*DOMESTIC** Cash and Interbank/Total Assets	-0.0461 (-0.39)	-0.0433 (-0.50)
*DOMESTIC** Loan Loss Provisions/Total Loans	**-1.8915* (-1.86)**	-1.1571 (-0.96)
*DOMESTIC** Equity/Total Assets	0.1778 (1.24)	0.1888 (1.55)
*DOMESTIC** Loans/Total Assets	0.1917 (0.75)	0.3247 (1.20)
*DOMESTIC** Other Earning Assets/Total Assets	-0.0854 (-0.59)	-0.0307 (-0.31)
*FOREIGN** Cash and Interbank/Total Assets	0.0137 (0.13)	0.0952 (1.08)
*FOREIGN** Loan Loss Provisions/Total Loans	-0.8248 (-1.25)	-0.4231 (-0.55)
*FOREIGN** Equity/Total Assets	**0.2829** (2.11)**	**0.3357*** (2.71)**
*FOREIGN** Loans/Total Assets	-0.0209 (-0.13)	**0.4136*** (2.61)**
*FOREIGN** Other Earning Assets/Total Assets	-0.1621 (-1.16)	0.0310 (0.28)
FOREIGN	-0.2726 (-0.81)	0.2516 (0.45)
MERGED	-0.1913 (-0.29)	-0.3788 (-0.70)
DC	**-0.3298*** (-3.54)**	-0.0398 (-0.46)
FOREIGN *DC	**0.2885*** (2.61)**	-0.1296 (-0.82)
MERGED *DC	-0.0368 (-0.23)	-0.0768 (-0.64)
Intercept	**-0.7216** (-2.51)**	**-1.8140*** (-4.28)**
R-squared	0.3398	0.2720
Number of Obs.	200	200
Number of Banks	23	23

Notes:
1) DOMESTIC Dependent variables and FOREIGN*Dependent variables are the interaction between domestic and foreign banks and independent variables respectively.
2) FOREIGN*DC and MERGED*DC are the interaction terms between foreign banks and post-crisis period and merged banks and post-crisis periods respectively.
3) The regressions are estimated by using ordinary least squared pooled cross-bank time-series data.
4) * denotes 10% level of significance, ** denotes 5% level of significance, and *** denotes 1% level of significance and t-statistics which are reported in the parentheses are calculated by using heteroscedasticity-corrected robust standard errors.

The regression 8 estimated from equation 4 reveals that the physical capital cost share of foreign banks is significantly positively related to equity and loans whereas that of domestic banks is unrelated to any independent variables. The estimated coefficients of the dummy variables for the ownership, the time effect dummy variables and interaction terms are all insignificant. The interpretation is that the physical capital inputs of the banks depend on banks' strategies and tend to be more long-term commitments. As a result, physical capital inputs are less flexible, which is also claimed by Kwan (2003).

3.5.3 Effects of Foreign Bank Entry through Acquisitions on Cost Efficiency

This section analyses the effect of foreign bank entry on banking efficiency in Thailand after the significant acquisitions by foreign banks in 1999. The same methodology as in 3.4.2 is applied in this section. In contrast to 3.5.1 and 3.5.2, the data set includes only nine domestic banks (representing both local private and state-owned banks) and four merged banks (representing banks with more than 50 per cent of foreign ownership since 1999) which represent foreign bank entry. The sample including only domestic and merged banks after the acquisitions allows me to compare banks which have similar business structures and customer bases. In fact, merged banks operate many businesses as domestic banks do. This enabled foreign banks to greatly expand their presence in the retail banking market through merged banks' branches and customer bases.

Table 3.5 presents regressions 9 and 10 which are estimated from equation 3. Both regressions provide very similar results. The findings show that per unit production costs of domestic banks are positively related to cash and inter-bank assets, loans and other earning assets; on the other hand, the costs of merged banks are negatively related to cash and inter-bank assets and other earning assets, illustrating that those domestic and merged banks have fairly similar business structures as expected. As for the domestic banks, loans are the most costly to handle, followed by cash and inter-bank assets and other earning assets. The estimated coefficients of the dummy variable for merged banks is insignificant, indicating that per unit production costs of domestic and merged banks between 1999 and 2003 are not significantly different. Regarding the time effect dummy variables, the estimated coefficient of acquiredyr is significantly negative, showing that per unit production costs of domestic banks after the acquisition year declined. The findings suggest that the cost efficiency of domestic banks improved. One possible reason for this is that greater foreign bank participation through acquisition increased the competitive pressure in the banking industry, and also to financial restructuring of domestic banks, which increased the cost efficiency of domestic banks.

Table 3.5: Regression Results (Panel B): The Comparison of Cost Efficiency of Domestic and Merged Banks: Total Operating Costs

Independent Variables	Dependent Variables:OPERATING COSTS	
	Regression 9 Operating costs/total assets	**Regression 10** Operating costs/total assets+deposits
	parameter t-stat	**parameter t-stat**
Cash and Interbank/Total Assets	**0.2251*** (4.10)**	**0.2299*** (3.44)**
Loan Loss Provisions/Total Loans	0.4695 (0.65)	0.4985 (0.65)
Equity/Total Assets	-0.0743 (-1.31)	-0.0793 (-1.28)
Loans/Total Assets	**0.5775*** (3.15)**	**0.4622** (2.23)**
Other Earning Assets/Total Assets	**0.1962*** (2.87)**	**0.1756** (2.51)**
*MERGED** Cash and Interbank/Total Assets	**-0.2624* (-1.67)**	**-0.2553* (-1.69)**
*MERGED** Loan Loss Provisions/Total Loans	-0.4616 (-0.54)	-0.5172 (-0.58)
*MERGED** Equity/Total Assets	0.3835 (1.25)	0.4170 (1.40)
*MERGED** Loans/Total Assets	-0.1183 (-0.37)	-0.0037 (-0.01)
*MERGED** Other Earning Assets/Total Assets	**-0.5552*** (-3.05)**	**-0.5718*** (-3.28)**
MERGED	-0.1683 (-0.18)	-0.0563 (-0.06)
acquiredyr	**-0.1865** (-2.31)**	**-0.2113*** (-2.61)**
MERGED *acquiredyr	-0.2009 (-0.76)	-0.1880 (-0.71)
Constant	**-2.7467*** (-7.57)**	**-3.4930*** (-9.11)**
R-squared	0.7066	0.7106
Number of Obs.	60	60
Number of Banks	13	13

Notes:
1) MERGED*independent variables are the interaction between merged and all independent variables.
2) The regressions are estimated by using ordinary least squared pooled cross-bank time-series data.
3) * denotes 10% level of significance, ** denotes 5% level of significance, and *** denotes 1% level of significance and t-statistics which are reported in the parentheses are calculated by using heteroscedasticity-corrected robust standard errors.

Table 3.6 shows the cost efficiency of domestic and merged banks in terms of labour costs (regression 11 and 12) and physical capital costs (regression 13 and 14). Regression 12 with higher r-square than regression 11 reveals that per unit labour costs of domestic banks are statistically positively related to cash and inter-bank assets, loan and other earning assets, whereas those of merged banks are statistically positively related to equity and negatively related to other earning assets. Interestingly, the findings illustrate that since the 1999 acquisition year merged banks focused on equity or quality of bank management and risk management in line with mother companies' directions. The estimated coefficients of merged, acquiredyr and of the interaction term of *MERGED*acquiredyr* are all insignificant, suggesting that the labour productivity of domestic and merged banks is indistinguishable during the period 1999-2003.

Table 3.6: Regression Results (Panel B): The Comparison of Cost Efficiency of Domestic and Merged Banks: Labour and Physical Capital Costs

Independent Variables	Dependent Variables:LABOUR COST		Dependent Variables:CAPITAL COST	
	Regression 11 Labour cost/total assets	Regression 12 Labour cost/total assets+deposits	Regression 13 Capital cost/total assets	Regression 14 Capital cost/total assets+deposits
	parameter t-stat	parameter t-stat	parameter t-stat	parameter t-stat
Cash and Interbank/Total Assets	**0.2890*** (4.40)**	**0.2638*** (3.91)**	**0.2314*** (3.65)**	**0.2061*** (3.26)**
Loan Loss Provisions/Total Loans	-0.3635 (-0.25)	-0.3345 (-0.23)	1.2211 (1.08)	1.2501 (1.13)
Equity/Total Assets	-0.0376 (-0.72)	-0.0425 (-0.76)	-0.0223 (-0.49)	-0.0272 (-0.56)
Loans/Total Assets	**0.8154*** (4.55)**	**0.7001*** (4.04)**	**0.8421*** (4.74)**	**0.7267*** (4.46)**
Other Earning Assets/Total Assets	**0.1595** (2.27)**	**0.1389** (2.01)**	**0.2240*** (2.75)**	**0.2035** (2.55)**
*MERGED** Cash and Interbank/Total Assets	-0.2890 (-1.47)	-0.2820 (-1.49)	**-0.2888* (-1.92)**	**-0.2817* (-1.95)**
*MERGED** Loan Loss Provisions/Total Loans	0.7785 (0.51)	0.7229 (0.48)	-1.4578 (-1.25)	-1.5135 (-1.32)
*MERGED** Equity/Total Assets	0.5538 (1.58)	**0.5873* (1.71)**	0.0433 (0.17)	0.0547 (0.19)
*MERGED** Loans/Total Assets	-0.2442 (-0.67)	-0.1295 (-0.37)	**-0.7364*** (-3.01)**	**-0.6217*** (2.75)**
*MERGED** Other Earning Assets/Total Assets	**-0.5875** (-2.50)**	**-0.6040*** (-2.69)**	**-0.4466** (-2.38)**	**-0.4632** (-2.54)**
MERGED	-0.1281 (-0.12)	-0.0161 (-0.02)	**-1.1565* (-1.79)**	**-1.0445* (-1.69)**
acquiredyr	-0.0814 (-0.71)	-0.1062 (-0.95)	-0.0063 (-0.08)	-0.0312 (-0.40)
MERGED *acquiredyr	0.1612 (0.62)	0.1742 (0.67)	-0.1596 (-0.67)	-0.1466 (-0.61)
Constant	**-3.8011*** (-11.13)**	**-4.5475*** (-13.41)**	**-4.4013*** (-12.56)**	**-5.1477*** (-15.16)**
R-squared	0.6604	0.6703	0.6956	0.7020
Number of Obs.	60	60	60	60
Number of Banks	13	13	13	13

Notes:
1) MERGED*independent variables are the interaction between merged and all independent variables.
2) The regressions are estimated by using ordinary least squared pooled cross-bank time-series data.
3) * denotes 10% level of significance, ** denotes 5% level of significance, and *** denotes 1% level of significance and t-statistics which are reported in the parentheses are calculated by using heteroscedasticity-corrected robust standard errors.

Regressions 13 and 14 show that the per unit of physical capital costs of both domestic and merged banks have the same pattern. In fact, these costs are related to cash and inter bank assets, loans and other earning assets. Interestingly, the physical capital cost regressions give broadly similar results as those of the total operating costs regression. The estimated coefficient of merged is significantly negative, suggesting that per unit of physical capital costs of merged banks are lower than those of domestic banks, in other words, the capital productivity of merged banks is higher than that of domestic banks.

Referring to the choice of inputs, regressions 15 and 16 (table 3.7) are estimated from equation 5. Regression 15 shows that after the acquisition year (2000-2003) the labour cost share of merged banks is higher than that of domestic banks during the same period. In contrast, regression 16 reveals that the physical capital cost share of domestic banks is higher than that of merged banks during the same period. The interpretation is that foreign bank entry leads to greater competition in the banking industry. Evidence of this is that domestic

Table 3.7: Regression Results (Panel B) of the Labour and Physical Capital Cost Shares of Domestic and Merged Banks

Independent Variables	Dependent Variables: Labour and Physical Capital Cost Shares	
	Regression 15 Labour cost/total operating costs	**Regression 16** Capital cost/total operating cost
	parameter t-stat	**parameter t-stat**
Cash and Interbank/Total Assets	0.0339 (0.48)	-0.0237 (-0.30)
Loan Loss Provisions/Total Loans	-0.8330 (-0.50)	0.7516 (0.75)
Equity/Total Assets	0.0368 (0.79)	0.0520 (0.96)
Loans/Total Assets	0.2379 (0.85)	0.2645 (0.89)
Other Earning Assets/Total Assets	-0.0367 (-0.50)	0.0278 (0.33)
*MERGED** Cash and Interbank/Total Assets	-0.0267 (-0.29)	-0.0264 (-0.28)
*MERGED** Loan Loss Provisions/Total Loans	1.2401 (0.74)	-0.9963 (-0.96)
*MERGED** Equity/Total Assets	0.1703 (1.16)	**-0.3401** (-2.38)**
*MERGED** Loans/Total Assets	-0.1258 (-0.42)	**-0.6180* (-1.93)**
*MERGED** Other Earning Assets/Total Assets	-0.0323 (-0.28)	0.1086 (0.97)
MERGED	0.0401 (0.06)	-0.9883 (-1.51)
acquiredyr	0.1050 (0.81)	**0.1801** (2.12)**
MERGED *acquiredyr	**0.3622** (2.28)**	0.0414 (0.21)
Constant	**-1.0545** (-2.49)**	**-1.6546*** (-3.43)**
R-squared	0.4221	0.2477
Number of Obs.	60	60
Number of Banks	13	13

Notes:
1) MERGED*independent variables are the interaction between merged and all independent variables.
2) The regressions are estimated by using ordinary least squared pooled cross-bank time-series data.
3) * denotes 10% level of significance, ** denotes 5% level of significance, and *** denotes 1% level of significance and t-statistics which are reported in the parentheses are calculated by using heteroscedasticity-corrected robust standard errors.

banks increased their physical capital costs resulting from financial restructuring in response to pressures exerted by foreign banks' entry through the acquisition (see also[21] Herberholz 2002).

[21] It is interesting that foreign bank entry through the acquisition of locally incorporated banks strongly affects the efficiency of domestic commercial banking systems than through the establishment of branches. The reasons for this include as follows; (1) generally foreign bank branches in Thailand do not compete on a level playing field and (2) access to retail banking seems to be heavily restricted (Herberholz, 2002).

3.6 Concluding Remarks

Using a bank-level dataset including 23 domestic, merged and foreign banks in Thailand, this paper analyses the development of per unit operating costs of the banking industry, compares the cost efficiency of domestic and foreign banks and examines the effect of foreign bank entry on banking efficiency in Thailand after the significant acquisitions by foreign banks after the 1997 financial crisis. Total operating costs consist of labour costs, physical capital costs and others and exclude the funding cost component which is assumed to significantly depend on domestic interest rates. The widely used translog cost functional form is used to estimate pooled regressions.

The empirical findings indicate that the production costs of domestic and foreign banks are different, illustrating that domestic and foreign banks are different in terms of business structures, management styles and customer bases. The foreign banks seemed to be more efficient than domestic banks in terms of better capitalisation and lower levels of nonperforming loans. In contrast, domestic banks concentrated on holding high levels of liquid assets. Unexpectedly, the unit costs of production of domestic and foreign banks are indistinguishable. In term of cost efficiency, foreign banks did not outperform domestic banks. A possible interpretation is that if foreign banks represent the best-practice banks in the industry, to a large extent, domestic banks in Thailand have managed to catch up to the best-practice standard.

Loans are more labour intensive than other earning assets. Surprisingly, there are fewer differences between the marginal labour costs with respect to other earning assets of domestic and foreign banks. On average the labour productivity of domestic, merged and foreign banks is indistinguishable. Regarding physical capital costs, domestic banks are more efficient in handling resale agreements and investments securities than foreign banks. On the other hand, foreign banks are more efficient in managing loans than domestic banks, a finding which may be due to either better monitoring systems and risk managements or better loan quality in their portfolios.

Regarding the effect of foreign bank entry through acquisitions on cost efficiency, the results show that per unit production costs of domestic banks after the acquisition year declined. This finding suggests that the cost efficiency of domestic banks improved, resulting from an increase in competition in banking industry arising from the foreign bank entry through acquisition. Since the 1999 acquisition year, merged banks focused on equity or quality of bank management and risk management in line with mother companies' directions.

Among seven countries in Asia, the observed operating costs of banks in the Philippines are highest, followed by South Korea, Indonesia, Thailand and Malaysia, compared to those of banks in Hong Kong. The unit costs of production between banks in Hong Kong and banks in Singapore are similar (Kwan, 2003). Combining these findings with this paper's results, policy implications can be drawn is that concerning foreign bank entry, domestic banks which have had to implement best business practices including on corporate governance can strengthen banks' competitiveness and complete with the new players.

Table 3.A.1: Indicators of Banking Systems in Thailand Classified by Types of Banks, between 1988-2003

	Pre- Crisis Period			Avg	Crisis Period	Avg	Post-Crisis Period	
	1988-90	1991-93	1994-96	Pre-crisis	1997	Post-crisis	1998-00	2001-03
Market Share (% of total)								
Total assets								
Domestic Banks	95.30	94.75	90.84	**93.63**	**80.63**	**88.18**	87.18	89.17
Foreign Banks	4.70	5.25	9.16	**6.37**	**19.37**	**11.82**	12.82	10.83
Loans								
Domestic Banks	94.96	94.68	92.50	**94.05**	**82.52**	**88.77**	87.82	89.72
Foreign Banks	5.04	5.32	7.50	**5.95**	**17.48**	**11.23**	12.18	10.28
Cash 1/								
Domestic Banks	96.37	94.78	87.79	**92.98**	**71.21**	**87.29**	86.28	88.29
Foreign Banks	3.63	5.22	12.21	**7.02**	**28.79**	**12.71**	13.72	11.71
Deposits								
Domestic Banks	97.85	97.88	98.27	**98.00**	**95.68**	**95.14**	95.48	94.79
Foreign Banks	2.15	2.12	1.73	**2.00**	**4.32**	**4.86**	4.52	5.21
Equity								
Domestic Banks	88.96	89.89	78.11	**85.65**	**31.12**	**48.92**	41.90	55.95
Foreign Banks	11.04	10.11	21.89	**14.35**	**68.88**	**51.08**	58.10	44.05
Total employment 2/								
Domestic Banks	n.a.	97.84	97.60	**97.72**	**96.75**	**95.78**	95.91	95.66
Foreign Banks	n.a.	2.16	2.40	**2.28**	**3.25**	**4.22**	4.09	4.34
Profitabilty: Operating Asset Ratios (% of total avg assets)								
Interest Margin								
Domestic Banks	n.a.	3.62	4.20	**3.91**	**3.60**	**1.36**	0.86	1.86
Foreign Banks	n.a.	3.75	3.45	**3.60**	**3.10**	**2.85**	3.29	2.41
Non-interest income (net)								
Domestic Banks	n.a.	1.06	1.31	**1.19**	**1.35**	**1.00**	0.91	1.10
Foreign Banks	n.a.	2.89	1.84	**2.37**	**1.57**	**1.86**	1.46	2.25
Gross income								
Domestic Banks	n.a.	4.69	5.51	**5.10**	**4.95**	**2.36**	1.76	2.96
Foreign Banks	n.a.	6.64	5.30	**5.97**	**4.67**	**4.71**	4.75	4.66
Pre-tax income								
Domestic Banks	n.a.	2.13	2.53	**2.33**	**-1.36**	**-2.34**	-4.88	0.21
Foreign Banks	n.a.	3.97	3.05	**3.51**	**1.31**	**1.00**	0.65	1.35
After-tax Income (ROA)								
Domestic Banks	n.a.	1.41	1.70	**1.55**	**-1.59**	**-1.68**	-4.15	0.79
Foreign Banks	n.a.	2.73	2.15	**2.44**	**0.78**	**0.54**	0.18	0.90

Source: The author's calculation from grouped data from Data Management Department, Bank of Thailand
1/ Cash includes cash and due from financial institutions and money market.
2/ Total employment is based on the figures at end-year.
3/ Net interest income is calculated by interest income and dividend substracting with interest expenses.
4/ Gross income includes net interest income and non-interest income.
5) Domestic banks include four merged banks which have more than 50% of foreign ownership.
6/ According to the International Loan Classification and Provision (LCP) rules and accounting standards by 2000. Recognition of occurred interest income was shortened from 12 months to 6 months and subsequently 3 months. As a result, banks faced huge increases in provisioning expenses since the introduction of these rules effective from end-December 1998. This led dramatic decrease in after-tax income.

Table 3.A.2: Indicators of Cost Variables in Banking Systems in Thailand Classified by Types of Banks, between 1988-2003

	Pre- Crisis Period			**Avg**	**Crisis Period**	**Avg**	**Post-Crisis Period**	
	1988-90	**1991-93**	**1994-96**	**Pre-crisis**	**1997**	**Post-crisis**	**1998-00**	**2001-03**
Ratio of total operating costs to total assets								
Domestic Banks 1/	n.a.	2.01	2.30	**2.16**	**2.58**	**2.28**	2.53	2.04
Foreign Banks	n.a.	2.46	1.99	**2.22**	**1.60**	**2.50**	2.18	2.82
Ratios of total labour cost 2/ tototl assets								
Domestic Banks	n.a.	0.93	1.03	**0.98**	**0.91**	**0.67**	0.70	0.65
Foreign Banks	n.a.	0.90	0.70	**0.80**	**0.42**	**0.65**	0.57	0.72
Ratios of total physical capital 3/ to total assets								
Domestic Banks	n.a.	0.35	0.40	**0.37**	**0.40**	**0.37**	0.37	0.37
Foreign Banks	n.a.	0.36	0.29	**0.33**	**0.16**	**0.23**	0.23	0.22
Ratio of loans 4/ to total assets								
Domestic Banks	82.09	88.43	101.14	**90.55**	**96.59**	**65.21**	67.23	63.19
Foreign Banks	88.23	93.76	91.49	**91.16**	**108.77**	**58.18**	59.57	56.79

Source: The author's calculation from grouped data from Data Management Department, Bank of Thailand

1/ Labour cost includes salaries and employee benefits.

2/ Physical capital cost includes premises and equipments.

3/ Loans are calculated by loans plus accrued interest receivables and minus allowance for possible loan losses.

Chapter 4 Dynamic Relationship between Financial Development and Economic Growth: A Regional Perspective

4.1 Introduction

In the aftermath of the 1997 Thai financial crisis, there were observable changes in Thailand's banking system. The subsequent decline in bank lending affected the effectiveness of the monetary transmission mechanism and eventually the formation of the monetary policy. In fact, both the long-run interest rate pass-through and the speed of adjustment of the 3-month deposit rate to changes of the minimum lending rate (MLR) declined significantly during the post-crisis period. At the same time, vector autoregression (VAR) models for Thailand reveal that the impact of monetary policy on output has weakened since 1999, and that this has been associated with a weaker bank-lending channel (Disyatat and Vongsinsirikul, 2003). These findings raise the question whether the financial development and the associated changes in the banking industry contributed to the economic performance or whether causality ran from economic performance to financial development. A related question is whether there are long-run effects of financial development on economic growth and whether bank-based or market-based financial systems are better for promoting long-run economic growth (Disyatat and Nakornthab, 2003).

Joseph Schumpeter argued already in 1911 (cited in Beck et al., 2000) that financial intermediaries play a crucial role in economic development in the sense that they select which firms should utilise society's savings. By doing so, financial intermediaries affect productivity growth and technological change. Another view is that better financial intermediaries can efficiently raise domestic savings rates and attract foreign capital, both of which ultimately contribute to growth. More recently, renewed attention has been given to exploring the possible linkage between the financial system and aggregate economic behaviour. This attention stems from the on-going beliefs of applied economists and policy-makers that financial markets and institutions play important roles in the growth and fluctuation of output (Gertler 1988). This recent empirical research confirmed that economies which have well-developed financial markets mostly posses high rates of economic growth. The question is whether there is a causal relationship, and if so, in what direction it is running.

Some recent research suggests that financial development has a positive effect on long-run economic growth (Bencivenga and Smith, 1991, Demetriades et al., 1998, Beck et al., 2000 a, b and Demirguc-Kunt and Levine eds. 2001). However, Beck et al. (2000b) argue that financial intermediary development may be not a cause of economic growth, but rather a leading indicator of growth. Jayaratne and Strahan (1996) go further by arguing that the observed correlation between financial markets and future growth may reflect a self-reinforcing feedback mechanism in which high growth economies might support bigger and more efficient financial systems, and these financial systems then in turn stimulate an economic growth spurt.

While the above cross-country studies generally find a positive relation between growth and financial development, there is less evidence on the effect of local financial development within the regions of a single country (Guiso et al., 2004) and the channels by which financial institutions affect the real sector (Jayaratne and Strahan, 1996). One reason may be the unavailability of data. This paper is intended to contribute to filling this gap. An advantage of examining the relationship between finance and growth in a regional perspective within a single country is that the region represents a more accurate definition of the relevant retail bank market (Valverde and Fernandez, 2004). In addition, all related institutional, legal and cultural factors are likely to be constant across regions within a country, thereby ensuring that differences in economic performance across regions are not driven by those factors. The present paper investigates the causality between economic development and financial development.

The paper proceeds as follows: in Section 4.2, it explores an important field in finance which is the finance-growth literature and the communities banking literature. Section 4.3 presents data and descriptive statistics and methodology. Section 4.4 presents empirical results and discusses the absolute convergence of economic growth across provinces and the conditional convergence of provincial economic growth with respect to financial development and other economic conditions and tests whether financial development affects provincial economic growth or the other way round. Section 5 summarises concluding comments.

The paper finds that the growth rates of real GPP per capita for 23 years between 1981 and 2003 are significantly negatively related to the initial level of real GPP per capita (1981) as expected from the growth theory. The results are also consistent with Barro and Sala-i-Martin's (1998) findings. When the initial level of real GPP per capita/worker is held constant, financial development variables significantly correlate with economic growth. Growth is positively related to the number of bank branches. Growth is statistically negatively related to deposits and unrelated to credits. Based on the Granger causality test results, there is a bi-directional causality between finance and growth, in other words, a feedback relationship as suggested by Demetriades and Andrianova (2003).

4.2 Conceptual Issues

This section explores an important field in finance which is the finance-growth literature and the communities banking literature.

4.2.1 Absolute and Conditional Convergence of Growth and Finance as a Source of Growth

Following Barro and Sala-i-Matin (1998), provinces, regions or countries which have lower starting values of capital/labour ratio k should in theory have higher per capita GDP growth rates and should tend to catch up and converge to those which have higher initial capital/labour ratios. The implication of this is that, all other characteristics of economies equal, per capita income of poor economies tends to grow faster than that of rich economies. This is referred to as `absolute convergence' (see figure 4.1). However, based on empirical data on growth rates and initial levels of real per capita GDP for 118 countries, the finding is that the growth rates are fundamentally unrelated to the initial positions. That is the hypothesis of absolute convergence does not hold for a broad cross section of countries. It does hold, though, for the 20 OECD countries and the states of the United States[1].

The transitional dynamics show how per capita income of an economy converges toward its own steady-state value and hence to the per capita incomes of other economies which are already in the steady state (see figure 4.1). The expression for the change in the capital stock can be found in Appendix 4.A.

However, the neoclassical model predicts that an economy converges towards its own steady state and that the speed of the convergence inversely relates to the distance from the steady state (Barro and Sala-i-Martin, 1998, p. 29). Hence the above conclusion depends on the assumption that all economies have the same parameters and therefore the same steady state positions. When this assumption is dropped, e.g. in the case of different savings rates, rich countries with higher levels of real capita GDP may be proportionately further from their steady-state positions, and their per capita GDP can grow faster than

Figure 4.1: Dynamics of the Solow-Swan model with technological progress

The growth rate of capital per effective worker ($(\hat{k} \equiv K/LA)$) is given by the vertical distance between the $s.f(\hat{k})/\hat{k}$ curve and the effective depreciation line, $(x+n+\delta)$, where s is the savings rate, f is output per effective worker, x is the constant growth rate of technological progress $A\ (t)$, n is the constant growth rate of population and δ is the capital depreciation rate. The economy is at the steady state when $\hat{k}$ is constant. Since $A\ (t)$ grows at the constant rate x, the steady-state growth rate of capital per person, $\hat{k}$, also equals x (also see

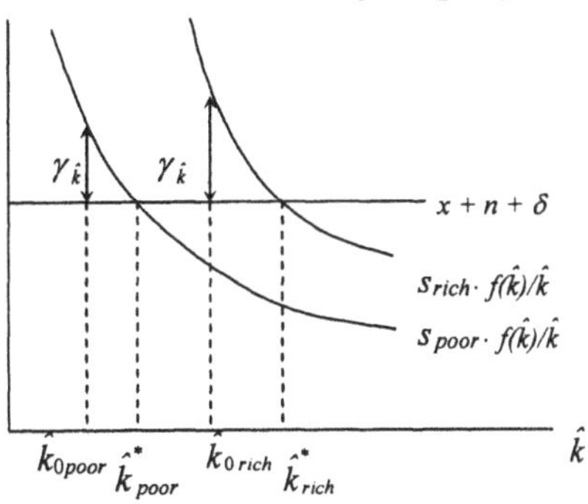

[1] see details in chapter 1: Growth models with exogenous saving rates (The Solow-Swan Model) in Barro and Sala-i-Martin (1998).

appendix 4.A). Source: Barro and Sala-i-Matin (1998)

Figure 4.2: Conditional Convergence

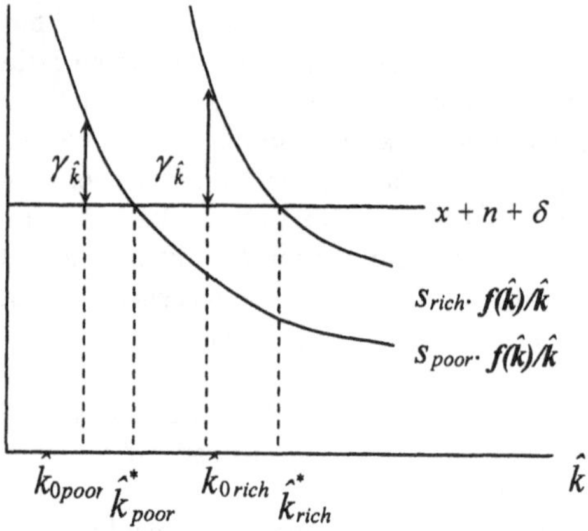

If a rich economy has a higher saving rate than a poor economy, then the rich economy may be proportionately further from its steady-state position. In this case, the rich economy would be predicted to grow faster per capita than the poor economy; that is, absolute β convergence would not hold.
Source: Barro and Sala-i-Matin (1998)

that of poor countries. This leads to the concept of `conditional convergence', (see figure 4.2) i.e. convergence conditional on controlling for differences in the ratio of gross investment to GDP and the initial quantity of human capital in the form of educational attainment and health.

Absolute convergence,[2] which is the hypothesis that poorer countries grow faster than richer countries and at last catch up with the latter, is one of the central issues discussed in the neoclassical growth theory arising from its property of diminishing returns to capital. It is claimed that the assumption of identical production technologies is not appropriate, and it is suggested that 'Solow growth models should be complemented with a theory of aggregate production differences with an aim of fully explaining international growth patterns (Durlauf and Johnson, 1995 cited in Islam, 1999). International comparisons of total factor productivity growth (TFP) based on results from three different approaches[3] reveal both similarities and discrepancies. The discrepancies of the results can play a complementary role in helping us to understand important issues of technological diffusion and TFP convergence (Islam, 1999).

[2] There are two main processes needed for income-convergence to be reached: (1) reaching similar levels of capital and (2) achieving similar levels of technology (Durlauf and Johnson, 1995 cited in Islam, 1999).

[3] Three different approaches include time-series growth accounting approach, cross-section growth accounting approach, and panel regression approach.

4.2.2 Causal Relationship between Financial Development and Growth

So far the economic growth theory in terms of absolute and conditional convergence has been discussed. The question studied in this paper is what are the linkages between finance and growth? Does finance[4] matter, i.e. is finance one of the variables on which convergence is conditional? The effects of finance can happen in the short run as cyclical and in the long run as changing the level of investment and its composition (Wallich, 1969). The debate on this issue can be divided into two broad channels. One channel is that improved financial intermediation increases the level of investment. When the financial sector is developed, savings can be efficiently mobilised and translated into investment. The other channel of the linkages between finance and economic growth is that better financial intermediation improves the efficiency of investment rather increasing the level of investment. Demetriades and Andrianova (2003) by contrast argue that financial development is, at the most, a facilitator of economic growth, rather than its ultimate true cause. They futher pointed out that finance is a necessary factor in processing new ideas into new products, services and technologies, and in exploiting natural resources.

The link between financial development and economic growth is not a recent finding. Interestingly, macroeconomists normally question whether financial factors definitely matter for growth. At the same time, almost all economic historians have little doubt about it and question instead how and how much they matter (Rousseau, 2003). Based on standard macro-econometric techniques and the historical time series of Amsterdam (1640-1794), England (1720-1850), the United States (1790-1850) and Meiji Japan (1880-1913), Rousseau and Sylla (2001) and Rousseau[5] (2003) showed statistical evidence that the development of banking and securities markets mattered for industrialisation and the expansion of commerce in four economies which have experienced 'financial revolutions' over the past 400 years. Gertler (1988)

---

[4] Wallich (1969) gave a very interesting explanation of the importance of finance: "...with a little imagination, this view of FINANCE may be linked to a large river of savings flowing into the sea of investment through a delta consisting of complex and frequently shifting arms and branches representing markets, intermediaries, and financial instruments. The flow in the river is determined largely exogenously. Total investment is not much altered by shifting flows carried by the various branches. But the welfare of the people living on the river banks, particular sectors in need of financing, savers, and the intermediaries facilitating the financing, is clearly affected.

[5] Rousseau (2002) asserted that most of the empirical growth literature underemphasised a vital mechanism through which finance plays an active role in the early stages of economic development. Finance acts as resource mobilisation. Banks and financial markets not only promote growth by aiming resources to productive sectors but also through their ability to take over project indivisibilities and to stimulate investors willing to accept longer time horizons for payoffs. Finance thus releases the first bottleneck problem which a young economy needs to pass.

pointed out that the main real and financial interaction in conventional Keynesian, Monetarist and Classical models emphasises the activity in the market for medium of exchange, rather than the markets for borrowing and lending. Lately, more interest has been focused on examining the relationship between the financial system and aggregate economic behaviour. Gertler's (1988) study of the recent literature on the real and financial interaction concluded that information problems normally decrease the market activity at the same time as they increase its sensitivity to disturbances, for example, to changes in interest rate or productivity. Institutions and financial contracts are determined simultaneously with real sector variables. Financial variables, for example, balance sheets positions and cash flow, affect individuals' and firms' expenses decisions, which finally generate income-accelerator effects on aggregate demand.

Much past work (for example; King and Levine, 1993, Rousseau, 2002, Rousseau and Sylla, 2001 and Beck et al., 2000a) shows that the level of financial development is a good forecaster of economic growth. One of the most influential papers in recent literature in this field by King and Levine (1993) showed results based on a study of 80 countries over 1960-1989 periods illustrating that indicators of the level of financial development, namely the size of the formal financial intermediary sector relative to GDP, the importance of banks relative to the central bank, the percentage of credit allocate to private firms, and the ratio of credit granted to private firms to GDP, are strongly and robustly correlated with GDP growth, the rate of physical capital accumulation, and improvements in the efficiency of capital allocation. In addition, the predetermined component of financial development is a good predictor of long-term growth over the next 10 to 30 years. In short, the standard statement of the Schumpeterian vision of 'creative destruction[6] may have been right about the importance of finance for economic growth (King and Levine, 1993: p.735).

Beck et al. (2000a) examined the impact of financial development on the sources of economic growth. The study is based on a cross-country sample with data averaged over the period 1960-1995 and uses two econometric procedures --a pure cross-sectional instrumental variable estimator and a Generalised-Method-of-Moments (GMM) dynamic panel technique-- which control for biases associated with simultaneity[7] and unobserved country-specific effects. They find that financial intermediaries provide a positive impact on total factor productivity growth which at last affects overall GDP growth. But the long-run

---

[6] Creative destruction is a process by which invention and innovation replace old production methods and goods with better procedures, commodities, and services (cited in King and Levine, 1993).

[7] The simultaneity bias may occur from the joint determination of financial intermediary development and (1) private savings rates, (2) capital accumulation, (3) total factor productivity growth, and (4) overall real per capita GDP growth (Beck et al., 2000, p. 263).

links between financial intermediary development and physical capital growth and private savings rates are questionable. Demetriades et al. (1998) found that financial policies namely interest controls, directed credit programmes and reserve and liquidity requirements, have a statistically significant influence on the average productivity of capital in five South East Asian economies, namely India, South Korea, Sri Lanka, the Philippines and Thailand. Using data of 21 developed nations and 28 developing nations between 1993 and 2000, Berger et al. (2004) found that greater market shares for community banks and efficiency ranks of small, private, domestically owed banks are associated with better economic performance, and the marginal benefits of higher shares for community banks are greater when these banks are more efficient.

Beck et al. (2000b) explored the links between financial structure --the degree to which a financial structure is market-or bank based[8] -- and economic development by using three different datasets; cross-country, industry and firm levels. Interestingly, the findings from those three different datasets and econometric methodologies give different views on the relationship between finance and growth. Some conclusions are that financial structure, i.e. the difference between market- or bank-based financial systems, does not explain economic growth, industrial performance or firm expansion, and the results seem inconsistent with both the market-based and bank-based views. By contrast, the evidence is likely to be consistent with the financial services and the law and finance views[9]. In fact, financial development and the legal protection of outside investors seem significant in explaining long-term cross-country growth rates. From the financial services point of view, financial development is important for economic development. By contrast, financial structure, per se, seems not to give more value added in explaining the process of economic growth. Ergungor (2003) proposed that financial system structure-- whether it is bank-based or market-based -- matters for economic growth. Markets-based financial systems seem to be better than banks-based systems in stimulating the economy in countries with flexible judicial systems. Interestingly, based on a study on cross-country differences in the legal rights of creditors, the efficiency of contract enforcement, and accounting system standards (the level of financial intermediary development), Levine et al. (2000)

[8] Beck at al. (2000b) stated that the bank-based view indicates the positive role of banks in mobilising resources, screening good projects, monitoring managers and managing risk. Importantly, even in countries with weak legal and accounting systems, powerful banks can influence firms to reveal financial information and pay their debts, thus supporting industrial development. The market-based view highlights the positive role of financial markets in promoting economic success in facilitating diversification of risks.

[9] The financial services view states that financial systems provide key financial services which are necessary for firms, industrial development and economic expansion. The law and finance view argues that the legal system is the primary factor behind the success of the financial system in promoting economic growth (Beck at al., 2000b).

found that legal and accounting reforms that strengthen creditor rights, contract enforcement, and accounting practices can enhance financial development and finally accelerate economic growth.

In spite of the progress in the growth literature, the issue of whether financial systems play any causal role in economic growth remains arguable. Probably, the reverse that high growth economies tend to produce large and privately funded financial systems may also be true (Jayaratne and Strahan, 1996). Wallich (1969) stated that the relationship between finance and the real sector does not run one way. We are likely to find primarily effects of finance on real variables. Nevertheless, the issue of causality does not seem to be discussed frequently (Levine et al., 2000). Demetriades and Andrianova[10] (2003) argued that normally we expect to see bi-directional Granger-causality, in other words, a feedback relationship between finance and growth. The causality can be reversed; economies with good prospects develop institutions to supply the funds necessary to support those good prospects. In short, the economy leads and finance follows (Robinson, 1952 cited in Jayaratne and Strahan, 1996).

4.2.3 The Relationship between Financial Development and Regional Growth

Valverde et al. (2004) pointed out the benefits of the regional perspective of the finance-growth nexus. The main contributions of a regional analysis can be summarised as follows; (1) heterogeneity across regions within a single country seems to be lower and more easily controlled for than across countries and (2) the exogenous factors of financial development, for example, the degree of liberalisation and the quality of the legal and institutional framework, which significantly affect the results, may be more efficiently controlled at the regional level than in a cross-country study[11]. One of a few studies using regional data within a country is Guiso et al. (2004). They showed that in Italy, a country which has been fully integrated in global financial markets for the last 140 years, local financial development matters for growth. The study suggested that under the condition of an increasing integration between Europe and the world, large firms will increasingly be unrelated to the conditions of the local financial system; on the other hand, small firms will continue to depend on it[12]. Hence

[10] At the same time, a well-functioning financial system is also expected to lead economic growth. However, it may be a case of no Granger-causality from finance to growth. Possible explanations can be, for example, the funds are allocated to non-productive projects owing to micro-economic inefficiencies in the banking system and political interference (Demetriades and Andrianova (2003).

[11] It is claimed that the link between intermediation and growth consists of the sum of multiple effects. A regional study may reveal some effects which are hidden in cross-country comparisons (Valverde et al., 2004).

[12] Ceteris paribus, in the case of Italy, a probability of an individual to be self-employed increases by 5.6 percent if he moves from the least financially developed region to the most

domestic financial institutions remain important even in a financially integrated Europe and world for some time to come. Based on 21 years (1972-1992) of banking sector data of the 50 states of United States of Americas, Jayaratne and Strahan (1996) found that the rates of real per capita growth in income and output significantly increased following the relaxation of bank branch restrictions. In addition, nonperforming loans declined significantly after branch restrictions were lifted. Banks do not lend more but they lend better. This seems to be the channel through which branching reform affects economic growth.

Valverde et al. (2004) estimated an AK model (or endogenous-growth model which is the absence of diminishing returns to capital) of economic growth with financial intermediation using a dynamic panel data analysis for 17 administrative regions of Spain over the period of 1986-2001. The results are consistent with results from cross-country studies, indicating that there is a positive and significant correlation between bank financial deepening and regional growth. The sources of financial development: product and service delivery innovations contribute positively to GDP, investment and gross savings growth. Valverde and Fernandez (2004) employed dynamic causality and panel data techniques on a sample of Spanish banks during 1993-1999 to analyse the link between financial deepening of banking activities on regional economic conditions and the direction of causality. The main results indicate that regional economic growth predicts financial deepening in the analysed period. With reference to bank dependence, the bank-lending plays an active role in the regions where households and firms are particularly dependent on bank credit.

4.3 Data and Descriptive Statistics and Methodology

This section describes the data and the definition of dependent and independent variables, as well as the empirical models.

4.3.1 Data and Descriptive Statistics

This paper is based on a newly available dataset. The dataset includes four parts. The first part is a panel sample for gross provincial product (GPP) and population (hereafter labelled population1) at constant 1988 price which is collected by the National Economic and Social Development (NESDB), from which GPP per capita can be calculated. The data are not obtained by representative unbiased surveys of industrial, agriculture and service sectors but are rather calculated by using value added based on a proxy variable. Provincial

---

financially developed one. On average, entrepreneurs are five years younger in the most financially developed region than in the least financially developed one. The ratio of new firms to population is 25 percent higher in the most financially developed province than in the least financially developed. Finally, per capita GDP grows 1.2 percent per annum faster in the most financially developed region than in the least financially developed one (Guiso et al., 2004: p.930).

income data are available for 72 provinces (Changwats) in Thailand for 23 years between 1981 and 2003; for the remaining four provinces,[13] the time series are somewhat shorter because these provinces were newly established according to a reform of provincial governments. GPP data[14] are part of the national income account compilation. In addition to GPP data, this part of the dataset also includes value-added by industry. The second part of the dataset includes the labour force data (population older than 13 years (prior to 2001) viz. older than 15 years (from 2001) between 1994 and 2003. This dataset also includes population (thereafter defined as population2), employment and working-age population by educational attainment. The third part contains information relating to financial development, including deposits, credits[15] and numbers of bank branches, all classified by provinces. Data between 1994 and 1998 come from unpublished data from the Bank of Thailand's library. A similar presentation of this dataset from 1999 onwards can directly be obtained from Bank of Thailand website. The data of deposits and credits are available in nominal terms; as a result, I divided them by headline consumer price index (2002=100) in order to obtain them in real term. The fourth part includes public and private investment which is used as proxies of capital investment in the models. The public investment is a part of the government budget distributed to each province except the capital city; Bangkok Metropolis since it has its own budget. The data are compiled by the Comptroller General's Department, Ministry of Finance. The department recently started to present this data by provinces; consequently, the series are rather short and comprise only 3 years between 2001 and 2003. As for the private investment classified by provinces, the data includes newly registered capital investment and recapitalisations of businesses registered at the Ministry of Commerce. The data of private investment[16] classified by provinces are available only for the Northern region

---

[13] The four provinces include Mukdahan, of which data are available since 1983, and Sa Kaew, Nong Bua Lum Phu and Am Nat Chareon, whose data are available since 1994.

[14] The GPP (Gross provincial product) data have been revised back to 1996 in accordance with the up-to-date set of data and indicators to be consistent with the national Gross Domestic Product (GDP) of 2003. See more details from

http://www.nesdb.go.th/econSocial/macro/nad/3_gpp/gpp2003.pdf .

GPP data from the year 1996 onward can be downloaded from

http://www.nesdb.go.th/econsocial/macro/macro_eng.php

[15] Deposits consist of current, savings and time deposits and others. Credits including out/in and out/out BIBFs (The Bangkok International Banking Facilities) consist of overdraft, loans and bills. See more details at

http://www.bot.or.th/bothomepage/databank/Financial_Institutions/New_Fin_Data/CB_Menu_E.htm

[16] Private investment data for 31 provinces of the Northern and Southern regions are collected only for registered capital investment and recapitalisation of firms registered at the Ministry of Commerce, rather total investment of the firms.

for 1996-2003 and for the Southern region for 1997-2003. The data are prepared by the Bank of Thailand regional offices (Northern regional office and Southern regional office).

Table 4.1: Descriptive Statistics

Variables	Mean	Std. Dev.	Min	Max	Obs.
Gross Provincial Products (GPP)	29,510.13	90,438.62	1,639.00	1,152,167.00	1,707
Population 1 1/	764,466	765,789	87,000	6,919,000	1,707
Growth GPP per capita 81-03	0.0389465	0.0865331	-0.3743691	0.7853191	1,631
Growth GPP per capita 94-03	0.0282614	0.1012459	-0.3590744	0.7947514	684
Growth GPP per worker 94-03	0.0278318	0.1388384	-0.5130477	0.7702389	684
FINANCE-Credits 2/	669.795	4,422.010	12.118	53,871.500	760
FINANCE-Deposits 2/	618.209	3,447.495	16.253	34,816.010	760
FINANCE-Branches 2/	45.203	120.282	4	1,259	760
LABOUR-Schooling 3/	69,266.130	97,608.050	5,569	1,017,544	760
LABOUR-Population 4/	809,831.200	885,825.700	131,693	8,079,343	760
CAPITAL-Public 5/	1,258.276	990.027	168	5,787	225
CAPITAL-Private 6/	979.498	2,942.187	0.00	40,669.00	231

Notes:
1/ Gross Provincial Products (GPP) at 1988 price from the National Economic and Social Development Board (NESDB).
2/ Credits including out/in and out/out BIBFs (The Bangkok International Banking Facilities) consist of overdraft, loans and bills. Deposits consist of current, savings and time deposits and others. Credits and deposits data are divided by headline consumer price index (2002) =100.
3/ Schooling represents working-age population in the education.
4/ Population figures are obtained from survey data compiled by the National Statistics Office.
5/ The public investment is a part of the government budget distributed to each province except the capital city; Bangkok Metropolis since it has its own budget.
6/ Private investment data includes newly registered capital investment and recapitalisations of businesses registered at the Ministry of Commerce.

Descriptive statistics are illustrated in Table 4.1. It should be noted that there are four new provinces, Mukdahan, of which data are available since 1983 and the rest; namely, Sa Kaew, Nong Bua Lum Phu and Amnat Chareon, whose data are available since 1994. Figure 4.3 shows the movements of gross provincial product (GPP) per capita between 1981 and 2003. The average real GPP per capita increased since 1983 and it was at a peak in the year 1996. Then it declined in 1997-1998 as a result of the 1997 Thai financial crisis, and it has gradually increased since 1999. The Central region[17] including Bangkok has the highest real GPP per capita, followed by the Southern, Northern and North-

[17] It should be noted that Thailand can be divided into five main regions as follows: Bangkok Metropolis, Central (25 Provinces), Northern (17 provinces), North-Eastern (19 Provinces) and Southern (14 provinces) regions.

Eastern regions during 1983-2003. Real GPP per capita is likely to have diverged across regions during this period or is likely to diverge in the future.

Figure 4.3: Thailand's Gross provincial product per capita, 1981-2003

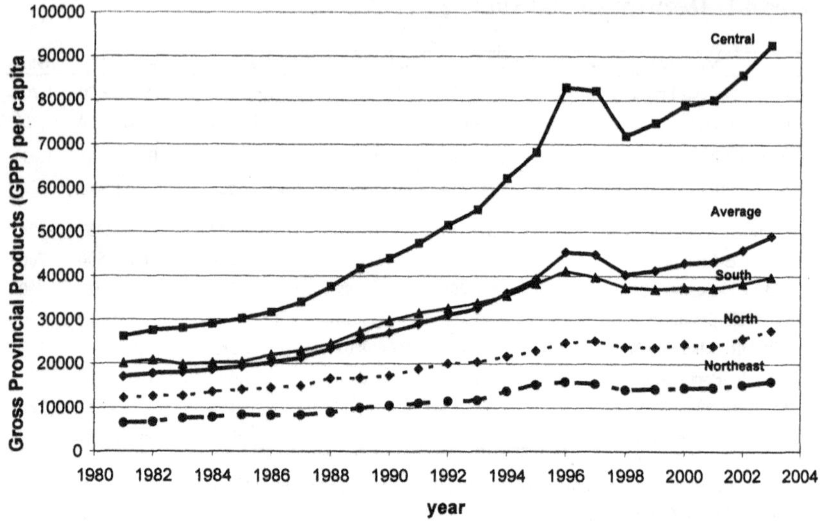

Figure 4.4 shows that credits in nominal terms taking write-off and write-back according to BOT's regulations into account slightly improved after 2001, when they were at the lowest level since the 1997 financial crisis. The improvement reflected the recovery in private investment when housing demand started to pick up, business sentiments improved and manufacturing production strongly grew. Similar to the real GPP per capita, credit distributed to the Central region including Bangkok were higher than those to other regions during 1994-2003. Historically, growth in real output has moved in tandem with credit. However, it should be kept in mind that as reported by IMF (2004) during the post crisis period non-bank sources of financing, which include trade finance, increased lending by Specialised Financial Institutions (SFIs), more recourse to capital markets and greater reliance on internal savings have supported growth.

Figure 4.4: Credit by Regions, 1994-2003

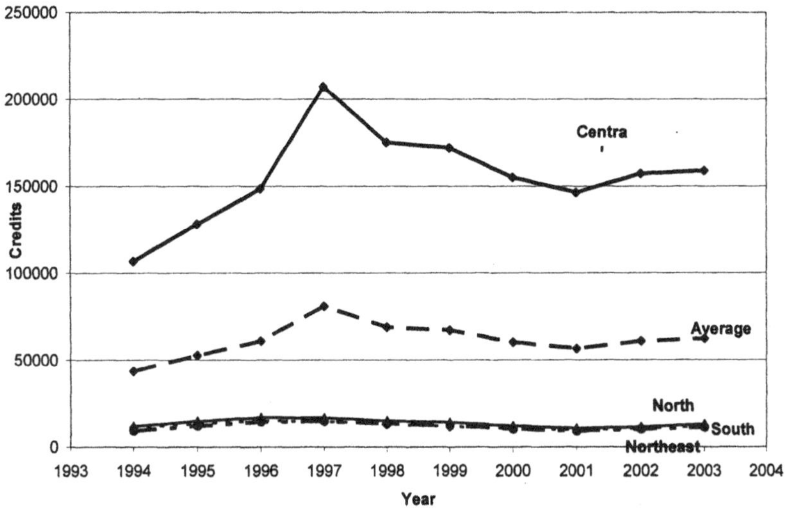

Figure 4.5: Deposit by Regions, 1994-2003

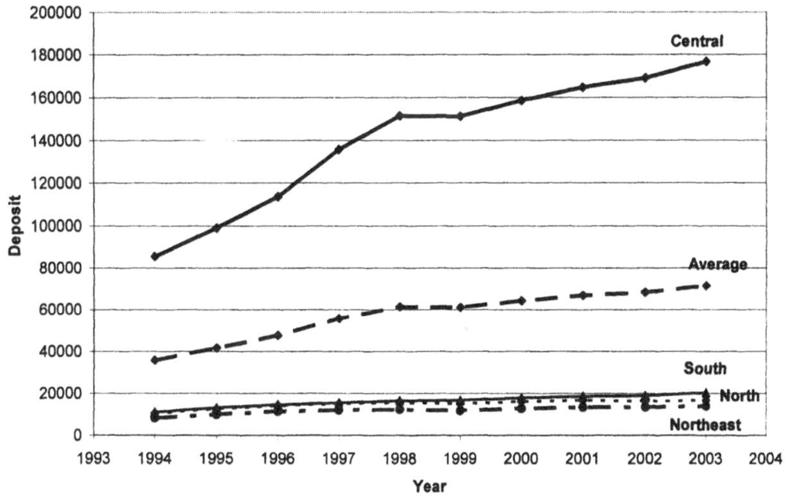

Figure 4.6: Bank Branches by Regions, 1994-2003

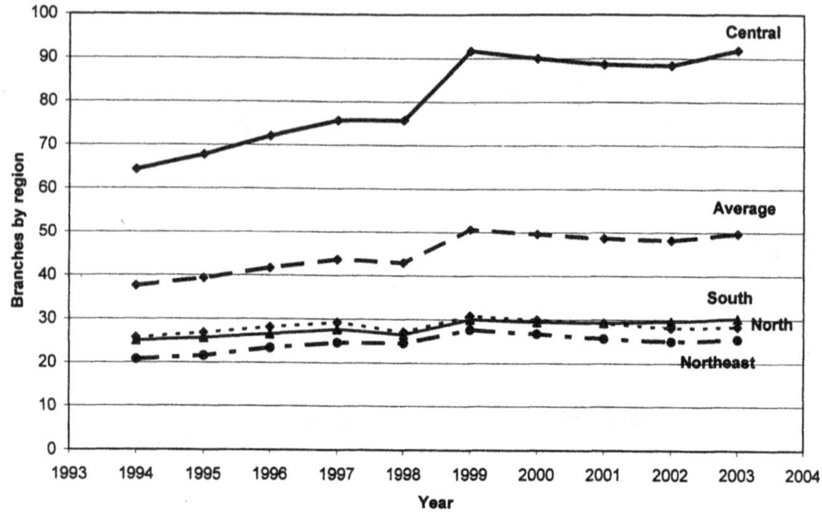

As for the saving mobilisation, figure 4.5 shows that deposits haves gradually increased since 1994 with a slight decline during 1998-1999. With reference to the number of bank branches, figure 4.6 presents that bank branches have continuously increased since 1994 with a noticeable increase during 1998-1999, resulting partly from the bank restructuring. Similar to credit distribution, deposits and branches concentrated in the Central region.

Figure 4.7: Credit and Deposit per Capita (Feb 2003)

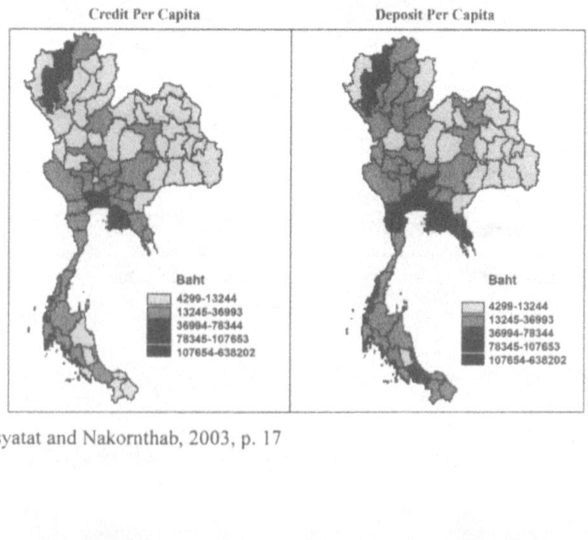

Source: Disyatat and Nakornthab, 2003, p. 17

Figure 4.8: Population per Branch (Feb 2003)

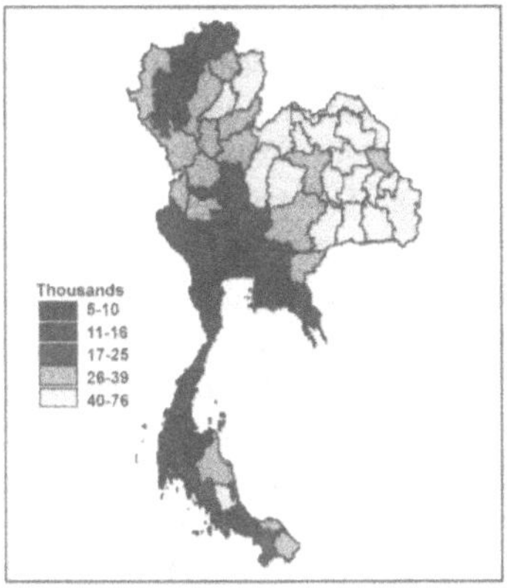

Source: Disyatat and Nakornthab, 2003, p. 18

With reference to the borrowing side, the left hand panel of Figure 4.7 suggests that much of the country, in particular provinces in the North-eastern region, remain under-supplied by commercial bank lending. On the other hand, the right hand panel of Figure 4.7 shows that from the saving mobilisation side, the situation seems to be less problematic. Figure 4.8 presents that the commercial bank branches concentrated in the Central and Southern regions, followed by the Northern and North-Eastern regions. The distribution of bank branches indicates that people in the North-Eastern region have less access to banking services (Disyatat and Nakornthab, 2003). Overall, Thailand could be regarded as under-branched with about 20,000 customers per bank branch, compared to about 1,500 in most developed countries (Herberholz, 2002).

4.3.2 Methodology

Demetriades and Andrianova (2003) suggested that there are two basic tests for the relationship between finance and economic growth. One is a test for a relationship between financial sector development and economic growth which has been used in much of the empirical literature on finance and growth for some time. The main finding is that even though the relationship is neither necessarily linear nor precisely estimated, the positive association between financial variables and economic growth is noticeable. The second is a Granger-causality test. In the light of the standard Granger causality definition, Granger (1969, cited in Rouvinen, 2002 and Hurlin and Venet, 2001) states that '...Y_t is causing X_t if we are better able to predict X_t using all available information than if the information apart from Y_t had been used.' Since the notion of 'all available information' is not operational, Granger's approach to regress X_t on its own lags and a set of lagged Y_t s has become the norm. If lagged Y_t s contribute statistically significantly to the explanation of X_t, Y_t Granger-causes X_t. It is interesting to see whether Granger causality runs from financial development to growth and/or vice versa.

4.3.2.1 Absolute and Conditional Convergence of Provincial Economic Growth

Following Barro and Sala-i-Martin (1998) and Klump (2003), the model specification for testing absolute and conditional convergence of provincial economic growth, both in term of gross provincial product per capita and gross provincial product per worker, proceeds from a Cobb-Douglas aggregate production function $Y_t = K_t^{\alpha}(L_t A_t)^{1-\alpha}$, where Y is output, K is capital, L is labour growing at an exponential rate n, and A is labour augmenting technology growing at an exponential rate of x (also see appendix 4.A.1). Following Klump (2003) and Guiso et al. (2004), controls for several factors are included in the analysis, namely initial GPP per capita/worker, the level of human capital which is measured by the educational attainment of the working-age population *(Schooling)*, the population *(Population)*, the public investment *(Pub Capital)* and the private investment *(Pri Capital)*. One of the differences between this paper and Klump (2003)'s paper is that this paper excludes structural parameters, for example, infrastructure and geographical advantages because of data unavailability. By contrast, the paper includes financial development variables which include deposits *(Deposits)* and credits *(Credits)* and numbers of bank branches *(Branches)* to test the link between finance and economic growth. Adjustyr is a time specific dummy variable to indicate the structural break in the data set. In fact, in 2003, there was a revision of Gross Provincial Product (GPP) data tracking back to 1996[18]. The study includes both a pooled cross-province, time-series analysis using data for different periods: 1981-2003, 1994-2003 and 2001-2003 and purely cross province analysis using data averaged over 1981-2003, 1994-2003 and 2001-2003.

The model specification for testing absolute and conditional convergence of provincial economic growth, both in a pooled cross-province, time-series and purely cross province analysis can be seen in the table 4.2.

---

[18] The GPP data series were revised in 2003 in order to be consistent with the following; (1) the economic indicators have been updated by the respective agencies collecting the data, (2) the national income account 2003 edition was revised, (3) the population number and structure of the Population Projections for Thailand 2002-2025 were revised.

Table 4.2: The Model Specification for Testing Absolute and Conditional Convergence of Provincial Economic Growth both a Pooled Cross-Province, Time-Series Analysis (Eqs.1-7) and a Purely Cross-Province Analysis (Eqs. 8-13)

Independent Variables (IVs)	**Dependent Variables**						
	GPP per capita Growth *ln (GPP per capita)$_{i,t}$ – ln (GPP per capita)$_{i,t-1}$*			**GPP per worker Growth** *ln (GPP per worker)$_{i,t}$ – ln (GPP per worker)$_{i,t-1}$*			
	Eqs.1 & 8	**Eq.2**	**Eqs.3 & 9**	**Eqs.4 & 10**	**Eqs.5 & 11**	**Eqs.6 & 12**	**Eqs.7 & 13**
IV1*a*	β_1 *ln Initial level of GPP per capita$_i$ (1981)*	β_1 *ln Initial level of GPP per capita$_i$ (1981)*	β_1 *ln Initial level of GPP per capita$_i$ (1994)*				
IV1*b*				β_1 *ln Initial level of GPP per worker$_i$ (1994)*	β_1 *ln Initial level of GPP per worker$_i$ (1994)*	β_1 *ln Initial level of GPP per worker$_i$ (1994)*	β_1 *ln Initial level of GPP per worker$_i$ (1994)*
IV2 (Finance)			β_2 *ln Credits*	β_2 *ln Credits*	β_2 *ln Credits*	β_2 *ln Credits*	β_2 *ln Credits*
IV3 (Finance)			β_3 *ln Deposits*	β_3 *ln Deposits*	β_3 *ln Deposits*	β_3 *ln Deposits*	β_3 *ln Deposits*
IV4 (Finance)			β_4 *ln Branches*	β_4 *ln Branches*	β_4 *ln Branches*	β_4 *ln Branches*	β_4 *ln Branches*
IV5 (Labour)			β_5 *ln Population*	β_5 *ln Population*	β_5 *ln Population*	β_5 *ln Population*	β_5 *ln Population*
IV6 (Labour)			β_6 *ln Schooling*	β_6 *ln Schooling*	β_6 *ln Schooling*	β_6 *ln Schooling*	β_6 *ln Schooling*
IV7 (Capital)					β_7 *ln Pub Capital*		β_7 *ln Pub Capital*
IV8 (Capital)							β_8 *ln Pri Capital*
Time Dummy variable		δ *adjustyr*	δ *adjustyr (in eq. 3)*	δ *adjustyr (in eq. 4)*			
Error Term	$\varepsilon_{i,t}$	$\varepsilon_{i,t}$	$\varepsilon_{i,t}$	$\varepsilon_{i,t}$	$\varepsilon_{i,t}$	$\varepsilon_{i,t}$	$\varepsilon_{i,t}$
Periods	1981-03	1981-03	1994-03	1994-03	2001-03	2001-03	2001-03

4.3.2.2 Financial Development and Provincial Economic Growth: Granger Causality Tests in Panel Data

The methodology applied in this paper is the Granger causality test also used by Hurlin and Venet (2001), Rouvinen (2002), and Valverde and Fernandez (2004).[19] It involves to estimate the correlation of the growth in GPP per capita and financial development (FDs) indicators which include credits giving across provinces *(Credits)* , deposits across provinces *(Deposits)*, and number of bank branches in each province *(Branches)*, and to include lags of the RHS variables as suggested by Granger (1969, cited in Rouvinen, 2002 and Hurlin and Venet, 2001).

Two conditions need to be fulfilled for financial development to Granger-cause or predict GPP (Valverde and Fernandez (2004):

1) Financial Development Indicators (FDs) are significant (employing an F-test) when FDs are included in a regression of the GPP as follows:

$$GPP_t = \alpha_0 + \Sigma\beta_i GPP_{t-i} + \Sigma\gamma_i FD_{t-i} \quad (14)$$

2) The GPP variable is not significant (employing an F-test) when GPP is included in a time-series regression of the corresponding financial development indicators (FDs) as follows:

$$FD_t = \alpha_0 + \Sigma\gamma_i FD_{t-i} + \Sigma\beta_i\, GPP_{t-i} \quad (15)$$

If the conditions are reversed, i.e. $\Sigma\gamma_i$ in equation 14 is not significant while at the same time $\Sigma\beta_i$ in equation 15 is significant, then provincial economic growth Granger-causes financial development. If $\Sigma\gamma_i$ in equation 14 and $\Sigma\beta_i$ in equation 15 are both significant, this indicates that the predictability occurs in both directions and probably, a third factor explains both GPP and financial development. However, individual fixed effects should be included in the empirical regression model (Holtz-Eakin et al. 1988 cited in Valverde and Fernandez, 2004):

$$GPP_{it} = \alpha_t + \Sigma_{l=1}^{m}\beta_{lt} GPP_{it-l} + \Sigma_{l=1}^{m}\delta_{lt} FD_{it-l} + \psi_i f_i + u_{it} \quad (16)$$

where i = 1,..., N; and t=1,..., T: f_i is the unobserved individual effect.

$$GPP_{it} - GPP_{it-1} = \alpha_t + \Sigma_{l=1}^{m}\beta_l(GPP_{it-l} - GPP_{it-l-1}) + \Sigma_{l=1}^{m}\delta_{lt}(FD_{it-l} - FD_{it-l-1}) + v_{it} \quad (17)$$

[19] Valverde and Fernandez (2004) tested Granger predictability between regional economic growth (GRGDP) and five financial deepening variables which include outstanding bank loans (LOAN), deposits (DEP), securities (SEC), the estimation of fee-earning activities (CBA), mutual funds (MF), and competition indicators; the Lerner index (LERNER) and a deposits market Herfindahl-Hirschman concentration ratio (HHI).

Equation 17 is derived from equation 16 by first-differencing to remove the individual effects from the model. Then, the estimation procedure of two-stage least squares (2SLS) with the instrumental variables is applied. The paper uses an extension of the Granger's causality test (1969, cited in Rouvinen, 2002 and Hurlin and Venet, 2001).) to panel data models with fixed coefficients (fixed-effects estimator from linear model with endogenous covariates)[20].

Dynamic fixed-effects models are biased in small samples. As a result, the appropriate corrections based convergent estimators, namely, Generalised Method of Moments (GMM) estimators (see Arellano and Bond, 1991) and IV estimator (Anderson and Hsiao, 1982) are also applied as suggested by Hurlin and Venet, 2001. Arellano and Bond (1991) introduced a GMM estimator for a dynamic first-differenced panel data equation, where all possible lags of regressors are used as instruments. At the same time, the Anderson and Hsiao estimator, which is estimated from the first-differenced model with either lagged levels or differences as instruments by two stage least squares (2SLS), is consistent as $N \rightarrow \infty$ (Anderson and Hsiao, 1981 and 1982 quoted in Rouvinen, 2002). As suggested by Hall et al. (1998), based on their experience with finite sample bias in GMM when the full set of orthogonality conditions is applied, a maximum of five lags is advisable. The present paper chooses three lags. I test for causality with a joint coefficient test. The test of over-identifying restrictions which is the test of the instruments' validity is used for the fixed effects and GMM models.

4.4 Empirical Results

This section presents the empirical results on absolute and conditional convergence of provincial economic growth and on Granger causality between financial development and provincial economic growth.

4.4.1 Absolute and Conditional Convergence of Provincial Economic Growth

Results from regressions 1 and 2 from table 4.3 (a pooled cross-province, time-series analysis) and regression 8 from table 4.4 (purely cross province analysis) show that the growth rates of real GPP per capita for 23 years between 1981 and 2003 are significantly negatively related to the initial level of real GPP per capita as expected from the concept of absolute convergence in the growth theory. The results are also consistent with Barro and Sala-i-Martin's (1998) findings.

---

[20] The model with fixed coefficients is

$y_{i,t} = \sum_{k=1}^{p} \gamma^{k} + \sum_{k=0}^{p} \beta_{i}^{(k)} x_{i,t-k} + v_{i,t}$ with $p \in N$ and $v_{i,t} = \alpha_i + \varepsilon_{i,t}$, where $\varepsilon_{i,t}$ are $i.i.d.(o, \sigma_{\varepsilon}^{2})$

Table 4.3: Absolute and Conditional Convergence of GPP per capita/ worker in Thailand, 1981-2003; A Pooled Cross-Province, Time-Series Analysis

All variables are expressed in logs. Regressions 1-2 show the results of absolute convergence of GPP per capita. Regression 3-7 shows the results of conditional convergence of GPP per capita/worker. The dummy variable for the adjustment year: *adjustyr* is included in regressions 2-4. t-statistics are reported in parenthesis and are calculated by heteroskedasticity-corrected robust standard errors. ***, **, * denote 1%, 5 and 10 % level of significance, respectively.

	Dependent Variables						
	GPP per capita growth			**GPP per worker Growth**			
Independent Variables (IVs)	**Eq. 1** **parameter** **t-stat**	**Eq. 2** **parameter** **t-stat**	**Eq. 3** **parameter** **t-stat**	**Eq. 4** **parameter** **t-stat**	**Eq. 5** **parameter** **t-stat**	**Eq. 6** **parameter** **t-stat**	**Eq. 7** **parameter** **t-stat**
Initial level of GPP per capita 1981, 94	-0.0090*** (-18.45)	-0.0121*** (-23.08)	0.0265* (1.73)				
Initial level of GPP per woker 1994				0.0213 (1.35)	0.0364* (1.79)	0.0378* (1.90)	-0.0006 (-0.02)
FINANCE-Credits			0.0130 (1.03)	0.0257 (1.18)	0.0487* (1.94)	0.0479* (1.92)	0.1170** (2.34)
FINANCE-Deposits			-0.0277* (-1.73)	-0.0384* (-1.77)	-0.0795*** (-3.14)	-0.0780*** (-3.08)	-0.1349** (-2.32)
FINANCE-Branches			-0.0001 (-0.00)	-0.0094 (-0.36)	0.0211 (0.79)	0.0173 (0.69)	0.0005 (0.01)
LABOUR-Population			0.0492*** (4.51)	0.0128 (0.82)	-0.0001 (-0.01)	-0.0003 (-0.02)	-0.0165 (-0.74)
LABOUR-Schooling			-0.0354*** (-2.89)	0.0070 (0.34)	0.0270 (1.22)	0.0250 (1.12)	0.0361 (1.01)
CAPITAL-Public					-0.0053 (-0.55)		-0.0008 (-0.05)
CAPITAL-Private							0.0033 (0.41)
adjustyr		-0.0358*** (-7.57)	-0.0812*** (-8.22)	-0.0602*** (-3.94)			
R-square	0.1642	0.1978	0.1490	0.0685	0.1367	0.1359	0.2427
Periods	1981-2003	1981-2003	1994-2003	1994-2003	2001-2003	2001-2003	2001-2003
Number of Obs.	1631	1631	684	684	225	225	91
No. of Provinces	72	72	76	76	75	75	31
Regions	C, N, NE and S	C, N, NE and S	C, N, NE and S	C, N, NE and S	C excluding BKK, N, NE and S 4/	C excluding BKK, N, NE and S 4/	N and S

Unlike the absolute convergence, models for conditional convergence consider additional possible determinants of growth across provinces (Klump, 2003). The relevant determinants in this paper include financial development variables: credits, deposits, the number of branches, human capital across provinces, the population and public and private capital. With reference to a cross-province, time-series analysis (equations 3-7 of table 4.3) and a purely cross-province analysis (equations 9-13 of table 4.4), the coefficients on the initial level of real GPP per capita/worker are positive in 8 out of 10 equations. The results suggest that there was no conditional convergence of real GPP per capita/worker in Thailand during 1994-2003. On top of this, in four out of 8 equations the initial level of real GPP per capita/worker was significantly positively related to growth which contradicts the results in King and Levine (1993) and Barro and Sala-i-Martin (1998). The results show that it is likely that

Table 4.4: Absolute and Conditional Convergence of GPP per capita/ worker in Thailand 1981-2003; Purely Cross-Province Analysis

All variables are expressed in logs. In contrast to regression 1-7, results from regressions 8-13 use data averaged over the period 1981-2003, 1994-2003 and 2001-2003 as indicated. Regression 8 shows the results of absolute convergence of GPP per capita. Regressions 9-13 show the results of conditional convergence of GPP per capita/worker. t-statistics are reported in parenthesis and are calculated by heteroskedasticity-corrected robust standard errors. ***, **, * denote 1%, 5 and 10 % level of significance, respectively.

Independent Variables	Dependent Variables					
	AVG GPP per capita growth		AVG GPP per worker Growth			
	Eq. 8	Eq. 9	Eq. 10	Eq. 11	Eq. 12	Eq. 13
	parameter t-stat	parameter t-stat	parameter t-stat	parameter t-stat	parameter t-stat	parameter t-stat
Initial level of GPP per capita 1981, 1994	-0.0092*** (-15.45)	0.0314** (2.16)				
Initial level of GPP per woker 1994			0.0181 (1.33)	0.0170 (1.24)	0.0169 (1.24)	-0.0237 (-1.54)
FINANCE-AVG Credits		-0.0113 (-0.67)	-0.0111 (-0.62)	0.0056 (0.36)	0.0059 (0.37)	0.0577** (2.47)
FINANCE-AVG Deposits		-0.0281 (-1.64)	-0.0327* (-1.73)	-0.0381* (-1.91)	-0.0385** (-2.01)	-0.0573** (-2.15)
FINANCE-AVG Branches		0.0255 (1.24)	0.0383* (1.70)	0.0316 (1.37)	0.0321 (1.56)	-0.0005 (-0.03)
LABOUR-AVG Population		0.0231** (2.28)	0.0147 (1.28)	0.0090 (0.87)	0.0087 (0.85)	0.0013 (0.08)
LABOUR-AVG Schooling		-0.0051 (-0.37)	-0.0021 (-0.13)	0.0014 (0.09)	0.0021 (0.14)	-0.0032 (-0.12)
CAPITAL-AVG Public				0.0009 (0.10)		-0.0075 (-0.61)
CAPITAL-AVG Private						0.0058 (0.79)
R-square	0.7471	0.5273	0.4776	0.4996	0.4995	0.7354
Periods	1981-2003	1994-2003	1994-2003	2001-2003	2001-2003	2001-2003
No. of Obs.	72	76	76	75	75	31
No. of Provinces	72	76	76	75	75	31
Regions	C, N, NE and S	C, N, NE and S	C, N, NE and S	C excluding BKK, N, NE and S 3/	C excluding BKK, N, NE and S 3/	N and S

there was divergence of real GPP per capita/worker in Thailand during 1994-2003, illustrating that when taking financial development and other related variables into account, the richer ones grew faster.

When the initial level of real GPP per capita/worker is held constant, some financial development variables significantly correlate with economic growth. Although the three financial development variables are highly correlated, I ran regressions with many combinations; the results are not qualitatively different from the presented ones in the paper. Growth is statistically negatively related to deposits (equations 3-7 and equations 10-13). Based on results from equations 3-7 and equations 9-13, neither for credits nor for branches could a robust correlation with growth be established. One possible reason for this is that there are other financial service providers[21] at the provincial level, and the most important one is a Specialised Financial Institution (SFIs), namely, the Bank for Agriculture and Agricultural Co-operatives (BAAC)[22], financial data of which are not included in this study. In fact, lending by specialised financial institutions has considerably increased since the 1997 Thai financial crisis (IMF, 2004). In spite of its statistical insignificance, a possible explanation for the negative relationship between economic growth and credits in equations 9 and 10 is that those provinces that had experienced particularly rapid credit growth in 1994-1997, *i.e. before the crisis*, where hit particularly hard by the crisis and so experienced a bigger contraction of GPP in 1997-98 and a slower recovery thereafter. Relatedly, the negative coefficients are consistent with the notion that a lot of the credits extended before the crisis were invested in low-return projects. These findings conform with Disyatat and Nakornthab (2003) in that regional financial development plays an important role in economic success of an area, and there is much room to improve financial access and development of less developed regions across the country. However, to firmly establish whether causality indeed runs from financial development to economic development, we need to look at the results of the Granger causality tests (Section 4.4.2 below).

Regarding the effect of labour variables on economic growth, the results show that both the growth rate of the population *(Population)* and the growth rate of the working-age population in the education *(Schooling)* are not robustly correlated to economic growth per capita/worker. The results suggest that there is no significant impact of labour variables on economic growth.

---

[21] Other sources of finance in rural areas consist of co-operatives and associations which on-lend BAAC funds to low-income households in rural areas and informal finance which includes moneylenders, landlords, traders, farmers, input suppliers, friends and relatives (Disyatat and Nakornthab, 2003, p. 18).

[22] In 1966 the government established the Bank for Agriculture and Agricultural Cooperatives (BAAC) as a state enterprise under the jurisdiction of the Ministry of Finance. The BAAC's mission was to extend credit more widely, directly to individual farmers as well as through farmer institutions. See more details at:
http://www.baac.or.th/eng_baac/about/history/history.htm

Because of the unavailability of the public and private capital data by provinces for earlier years, the equations including these variables (i.e. 5, 7, 11 and 13) cover only three years from 2001-2003. Similar to the effect of labour variables on economic growth, results that capital variables have no robust effect on economic growth.

4.4.2 Financial Development and Provincial Economic Growth: Granger Causality Tests in Panel Data

There is a little doubt about the linkage between finance and growth in cross-country studies. This sub-section discusses the direction of causality between finance and growth in the provincial study in the case of Thailand.

Credits, bank branches and deposits are considered as proxies of the financial development. I test the Granger causality from the financial development to provincial economic growth and vice versa. The main results of the Granger causality tests are presented in tables 4.5 and 4.6. As can be seen from table 4.5, our three estimators, namely the fixed-effects estimator, the Anderson-Hsiao estimator and the Generalised Method of Moments (GMM) estimator give almost the same results. Almost all the F-tests support the joint significance of credits, bank branches and deposits in growth regressions. These results are robust for all three models; although the results of the Sargent test of overidentifying restrictions applied to the fixed-effects estimator and GMM estimator raise doubts about the validity of the instrumental variables. As expected, the observed results indicate that financial development Granger causes provincial economic growth, illustrating the importance of financial development, in particular, banking sector development, in affecting provincial economic growth. This may explain why Thailand's economy, which heavily relies upon bank-finance,[23] suffered so much economic contraction from the recent financial crises.

With reference to an inverse causality relationship from provincial economic growth to financial development, table 4.6 shows that the three estimators give the same results. In fact, all F-test for the joint significance of the parameters for cases of growth to credits, bank branches and deposits for the first three lags reject H_0 (H_0 = parameters jointly equal zero), implying inverse causality. This finding contradicts with Valverde and Fernandez (2004)'s work[24]

[23] The size of Thailand's banking sector relative to GDP is large, but not excessively large. Based on the ratio of commercial banks' claims on private sector to GDP of 22 countries averaged over 1997-2002, Thailand stood almost in the middle of the pack with a ratio of around 97 percent, higher than the average of 83 percent (Disyatat and Nakornthab (2003).

[24] However, they further illustrated that it does not mean that the financial sector cannot contribute to economic growth. They found that there are positive effects of commercial banks' lending on regional growth, illustrating that specialised intermediaries played active roles in regional markets in providing loans to disadvantaged groups.

indicating that only the inverse causality relationship for Spain during 1993-1999. The inverse causality relationship from growth to financial development suggests that the economic take off (or recession) generally occurs before the financial take off (or crash) (Hurlin and Venet, 2001).

These results suggest that there is two-way causality between finance and growth in Thailand during 1994-2003, in other words, a feedback relationship exists as suggested by Demetriades and Andrianova, 2003. Combining the recent work in the regional level with the paper's finding, it can be concluded that economic take off seems to be one of the main factors for financial take off for most of the countries. By contrast, the opposite causality from financial development to growth in the cross-country studies is true for most countries. This evidence confirms that the economic development does not follow the same path for heterogeneous countries (Hurlin and Venet (2001).

Table 4.5: Panel Data Granger Causality Tests (1), Financial Development and Provincial Economic Growth in Thailand, 1994-2003, 2 SLS with instrumental variables, 95% significance level

Causality from Financial Development to Provincial Economic Growth											
Fixed-Effects Estimator				Anderson-Hsiao Estimator				GMM estimator			
1) Credits causes GPP growth											
lags	F-test	Results	Obs.	lags	F-test	Results	Obs.	lags	F-test	Results	Obs.
1	133.00	yes	532	1	68.09	yes	456	1	673.46	yes	608
2	185.99	yes	532	2	115.26	yes	456	2	932.87	yes	532
3	189.44	yes	532	3	80.33	yes	456	3	337.77	yes	456
2) Branch causes GPP growth											
lags	F-test	Results	Obs.	lags	F-test	Results	Obs.	lags	F-test	Results	Obs.
1	0.10	no	532	1	21.06	yes	456	1	171.99	yes	608
2	10.01	yes	532	2	39.38	yes	456	2	164.13	yes	532
3	49.30	yes	532	3	37.53	yes	456	3	109.68	yes	456
3) Deposits causes GPP growth											
lags	F-test	Results	Obs.	lags	F-test	Results	Obs.	lags	F-test	Results	Obs.
1	19.52	yes	532	1	7.12	yes	456	1	289.24	yes	608
2	19.45	yes	532	2	8.17	yes	456	2	1010.5	yes	532
3	25.72	yes	532	3	67.53	yes	456	3	139.41	yes	456

Notes:
1) F-test is a test for the joint significance of the parameters.
2) Although the results of the Sargent test of overidentifying restrictions give doubt on the validity of the instrumental variables, the results of the F-test for the joint significance of the parameters are robust.

Table 4.6: Panel Data Granger Causality Tests (2), Financial Development and Provincial Economic Growth in Thailand, 1994-2003, 2 SLS with instrumental variables, 95% significance level

Causality from Provincial Economic Growth to Financial Development											
Fixed-Effects Estimator				Anderson-Hsiao Estimator				GMM estimator			
1) GPP growth causes Credits											
lags	F-test	Results	Obs.	lags	F-test	Results	Obs.	lags	F-test	Results	Obs.
1	93.67	yes	532	1	76.10	yes	456	1	593.05	yes	608
2	94.53	yes	532	2	70.33	yes	456	2	747.52	yes	532
3	121.63	yes	532	3	42.83	yes	456	3	388.84	yes	456
2) GPP growth causes Branch											
lags	F-test	Results	Obs.	lags	F-test	Results	Obs.	lags	F-test	Results	Obs.
1	15.46	yes	532	1	20.13	yes	456	1	7.27	yes	608
2	23.09	yes	532	2	41.59	yes	456	2	111.27	yes	532
3	28.00	yes	532	3	73.08	yes	456	3	246.73	yes	456
3) GPP growth causes Deposits											
lags	F-test	Results	Obs.	lags	F-test	Results	Obs.	lags	F-test	Results	Obs.
1	17.44	yes	532	1	36.77	yes	456	1	163.68	yes	608
2	39.11	yes	532	2	60.35	yes	456	2	299.52	yes	532
3	39.52	yes	532	3	91.64	yes	456	3	278.45	yes	456

Notes:
1) F-test is a test for the joint significance of the parameters.
2) Although the results of the Sargent test of overidentifying restrictions give doubt on the validity of the instrumental variables, the results of the F-test for the joint significance of the parameters are robust.

4.5 Concluding Comments

The paper finds that based on both a cross-province, time-series analysis and a purely cross-province analysis the growth rates of real GPP per capita for 23 years between 1981 and 2003 are significantly negatively related to the initial level of real GPP per capita (1981) as expected from the growth theory as indicated by Barro and Sala-i-Martin's (1998). However, when taking financial development and other related variables into account, the results show that the average growth rates of real GPP per capita for 10 years during 1994 to 2003 are significantly positively related to the starting level of real GPP per capita/worker suggesting that, after controlling for financial development, there is divergence of real GPP per capita/worker in Thailand during 1994-2003. The evidence illustrates that among provinces with the same financial development, the richer ones grew faster.

However, when the initial level of real GPP per capita/worker is held constant, neither credits nor branches robustly correlated with growth. One possible reason for this is that there are other financial service providers[25] at the

[25] Other sources of finance in rural areas consist of co-operatives and associations which on-lend BAAC funds to low-income households in rural areas and informal finance which

provincial level. The most important one is a Specialised Financial Institution (SFIs), namely, the Bank for Agriculture and Agricultural Co-operatives (BAAC)[26], financial data of which are not included in this study. Despite of statistical insignificance, one of the possible explanations for the negative relationship between economic growth and credits is that those provinces that had experienced particularly sharp credit growth in 1994-1997, *i.e. before the crisis*, experienced a bigger contraction of GPP in 1997-98 and a slower recovery thereafter. As for the effect of labour and capital variables on economic growth, the results show there is no robust effect of labour and capital variables on economic growth.

Based on the Granger causality test results, there is a bi-directional causality between finance and growth, in other words, a feedback relationship as suggested by Demetriades and Andrianova (2003). This evidence confirms that the economic development does not follow the same path for heterogeneous groups of countries (Hurlin and Venet (2001).

---

includes moneylenders, landlords, traders, farmers, input suppliers, friends and relatives (Disyatat and Nakornthab, 2003, p. 18).

[26] In 1966 the government established the Bank for Agriculture and Agricultural Cooperatives (BAAC) as a state enterprise under the jurisdiction of the Ministry of Finance. The BAAC's mission was to extend credit more widely, directly to individual farmers as well as through farmer institutions. See more details at:
http://www.baac.or.th/eng_baac/about/history/history.htm

Appendix

4.A.1 Mathematical Appendix

The summary of how to derive the steady state of the Solow-Swan Model with labour-augmenting technological progress is presented below. Let us assume that there are only two inputs; physical capital, *K(t)*, and labour, *L(t)*. The production function takes the form $Y(t) = F[K(t), L(t), t]$, where *Y(t)* is the flow of output produced at time *(t)*. The production function depends on time, *t*, to reflect the effects of technological progress. We assume a one-sector production technology in which output is a homogeneous good that can be consumed, *C(t)*, or invested, *I(t)*, to create new units of physical capital, *K(t)*. We assume that the economy is closed: households cannot buy foreign goods or assets and cannot sell home goods or assets abroad. As a result, in a closed economy, output equals income, and the amount invested equals the amount saved. Let $s(\bullet)$ be the saving rate and $1 - s(\bullet)$ the fraction of output that is consumed. We assume that $s(\bullet)$ is given exogenously. We use the constant-saving-rate specification. We assume that capital depreciates at the constant rate $\delta > 0$ (Barro and Sala-i-Martin, (1998).

The net increase in the stock of physical capital at a point in time equals gross investment less depreciation:

$$\dot{K} = I - \delta . K = s . F(K, L, t) - \delta . K \tag{1}$$

where a dot over a variable, for example, $\dot{K}$ denotes differentiation with respect to time and $0 \leq s \leq 1$. Equation 1 determines the dynamics of *K* for a given technology and labour force. Here, we neglect technological progress; that is, we assume that $F(\bullet)$ is independent of *t*. This assumption will be relaxed later. The labour force, *L*, varies over time because of population growth. We assume that population grows at a constant, exogenous rate, $\dot{L}/L = n >= 0$, with $L(t) = e^{nt}$. Then equation 1 determines the time paths of capital and output. Apparently, minor differences in assumptions about $F(\bullet)$ can generate different theories of economic growth. If we divide both sides of the equation by *L*, then we get

$$\dot{K}/L = s . f(k) - \delta . k \tag{2}$$

The right hand side includes per capita variables only; on the other hand the left-hand side does not. We can write $\dot{K}/L$, as a function of *k* by using the condition:

$$\dot{k} = \frac{d(K/L)}{dt} = \dot{K}/L - nk \tag{3}$$

where $n = \dot{L}/L$. If we substitute this product into the expression for $\dot{K}/L$ then we can rearrange terms to get:

$$\dot{k} + nk = s . f(k) - \delta . k$$

$$\dot{k} = s . f(k) - (n + \delta) . k \tag{4}$$

Equation 4 is the fundamental differential equation of the Solow-Swan model. This nonlinear equation depends only on *k*. The term $(n + \delta)$ on the right-hand side of equation 4 can be interpreted as the effective depreciation rate for the capital/labour ratio, $k = K/L$. If the saving rate, *s*, were 0, then *k* would decline partly due to depreciation of *K* at the rate δ and partly due to growth of *L* at the rate *n*.

Division of both sides of equation 4 by *k* implies that the growth rate of *k* is given by:

$$\gamma_k = \dot{k}/k = s.f(k)/k - (n+\delta) \qquad (5)$$

The steady state is the situation where the capital stock and the population grow at constant rates, i.e.where $\dot{k} = 0$: then k^* satisfies the condition

$$s.f(k^*) = (n+\delta).k^* \qquad (6)$$

Hence, in the neoclassic model, the per capita quantities *k, y* and *c* do not grow in the steady state. However, *K, Y and C* grow in the steady state at the rate of population growth *n*. Importantly, changes in the level of technology, the saving rate, the rate of population growth, and the depreciation rate do not affect the steady-state growth rates of per capita output, capital, and consumption, all of which are equal to zero. Consequently, the model does not give explanations of the determinants of long-run per capita growth.

As for the case of Solow-Swan Model with labour-augmenting technological progress, exogenous technological progress is introduced. Suppose we consider only constant rates of technological progress. Then, in the neoclassical growth model, only labour-augmenting technological change provides consistent existent of a steady state, of which growth rates of the various quantities in the long run are constant. (see proof in Barro and Sala-i-Martin, 1998). We assume that the production function includes labour-augmenting technological progress as shown in the equation; $Y = F[K, L \cdot A(t)]$ and that the technology term, $A(t)$, grows at the constant rate x. The condition for the change in the capital stock is

$$\dot{K} = s.F[K, L \cdot A(t)] - \delta.K \qquad (7)$$

Then, we do similar way as equations 2-4, then we get

$$\hat{\gamma}_k = \dot{\hat{k}}/\hat{k} = s.f(\hat{k})/\hat{k} - (x+n+\delta) \qquad (8)$$

Equation 8 is similar to equation 5. The only difference is that aside from the hat, is that the last term on the right-hand side includes the parameter x. The term $(x+n+\delta)$ is 'the effective depreciation rate for $\hat{k} \equiv K/\hat{L}$. If the saving rate, s, were 0, then $\hat{k}$ would decline partly due to depreciation of K at the rate δ and partly due to growth of $\hat{L}$ at the rate $x+n$. Because the steady-state growth rate of $\hat{k}$ is zero, the steady state can be presented as follows:

$$s.f(\hat{k}^*) = (x+n+\delta).\hat{k}^* \qquad (9)$$

The transitional dynamics of $\hat{k}$ are qualitatively similar to those of k in the Solow-Swan model.

...an old western saying 'an ounce of prevention is worth a pound of cure' which is similar to the old Thai saying 'Kunwei-deekua-ka'. As the experience from the Thai financial crisis shows, this wisdom is not old fashion; it is always applicable...

Chapter 5 Summary and Conclusions

Before the 1997 financial crisis, East Asian countries (i.e. Hong Kong, Indonesia, South Korea, Malaysia, Singapore, Taiwan and Thailand) were regarded as economic miracles. Regional economic growth during 1960-1995 had outpaced growth in other groups of developing countries. The 1997 banking and balance of payments crisis (twin crisis) revealed economic and political problems in the region and slowed down its growth to a certain extent. Bankers, economists and regulators everywhere agree that bank runs or failures are costly to the economy. Output losses during past banking crises have been on average large, over 10 percent of annual GDP. Importantly, the losses from banking crises in the developing countries tended to be large relative to income when compared to those in industrialised countries. Countries facing financial crises share some features ranging from cronyism, over-borrowing, panic by foreign investors, liberalisation with inadequate regulation, boom and bust cycles and external economic shocks. The main lesson from the study of crises in the late 1980s and early 1990s is that managing crises in emerging markets is much different than in industrial countries owing to the weaker financial institutions, larger degree of problems and different circumstances. As a result, best practice from industrial countries cannot be simply applied to developing countries.

This study contributes to answering several questions. What are the consequences of the 1997 Thai crisis for the banking sector? What are the policy implications? What can we do to prevent financial crises in the future? What happened to the Thai banking sector before the crisis? Why did its performance deteriorate so rapidly within a few years in the run-up to the crisis? Have financial development and the associated changes in the banking industry affected economic performance? Or does causality run from economic performance to financial development?

A twin crisis, i.e. the association of a bank and currency crisis may be attributable to three main channels of causation: a banking leading to a currency crisis, a currency leading to a banking crisis, or joint causality. As for the joint causality, there can be a close link between a country's currency stability and the health of its banking sector. Devaluation worsens the balance sheets of finance intermediaries which lead to a pronounced tightening in credit market conditions and possibly to a contraction in output. The adverse consequences of a devaluation are even worse if banks' balance sheets are deteriorated by non-performing loans (NPLs), or if banks hold large amounts of foreign liabilities at short horizons. Consequently, banking and currency crises can amplify each other and generate a vicious circle. The leading explanations of the Asian twin crisis include the well-know `moral hazard' problems in banking in association with financial liberalisation and government deposit insurance; and large macroeconomic shocks. The Asian banking and financial systems were fragile both in terms of inefficient supervision and regulation already before the onset of the crisis. As for Thailand, a large number of Thai financial institutions were distressed since the first half of 1997. Troubled financial institutions which concentrated their lending in real estate and property were financed by borrowing from foreign financial institutions. By about the end of June 1997, the Bank of Thailand had committed US$ 28 billions out of US$ 30 billions in international reserves in forward market interventions for defending the value of the baht. On July 2, 1997, Thailand announced a managed float of the Baht and began to negotiate a rescue programme with the IMF. Finally, 58 finance companies went bankrupt and were forced to close. During the 1997 financial crisis, the Thai economy contracted, and banks faced severe liquidity shortages and a sharp deterioration in the quality of their assets.

The authorities implemented various policy measures in order to reform and rehabilitate the financial system in accordance with the conditions of the IMF programme. Besides the major monetary and fiscal tightening and external balance policies, the programme included four core objectives: to strengthen the financial system, to improve governance and transparency, to restore economic competitiveness, and to modernise the legal and regulatory environment. With reference to the consequences for the banking sector after the crisis, there are four main findings. Firstly, the improvements in banks' balance sheets have been reflected in the decline in the level of NPLs; however, the large overhang of NPLs still has not been fully removed. At the same time, bank capitalisation has significantly improved. Secondly, the credit channel of monetary transmission was impaired by the crisis. Bank-lending rates adjusted slowly and private credit grew slowly. The collapse of banks in the crisis had a strong effect on GDP. Thirdly, the financial structure of Thailand has changed since the crisis. In particular, bank credit declined (bank disintermediation). The decline in bank lending is attributed to more strict regulations, in particular, higher capital adequacy requirements. Domestic commercial banks in Thailand seem to be more affected by these regulations than foreign bank branches. In response to this, banks have been restructuring their strategies by diversifying their customer bases and scope of activities. Lastly, a widespread episode called `flight to quality' during the Thai financial crisis was observable. Depositors in Thailand shifted funds from finance companies and small banks towards larger banks, particularly foreign financial institutions. As for the ownership structure, before the 1997 financial crisis, all locally-incorporated banks in Thailand were majority owned by Thai citizens. After the crisis, at the end of 1999, 4 out of 13 locally-incorporated banks turned to be majority-owned by foreigners.

After the 1997 financial crisis, the worst in Thailand's history, Thailand has worked to build a sustainable economy based upon a safe and sound financial sector. However, there are still major challenges ahead. Some lessons from the crisis can be drawn. One focuses on how to solve a crisis once it happens. The emphasis should be on the strategies in the closure of nonviable financial companies and bank and corporate debt restructuring. What are needed are quick responses, and clear and well-sequenced procedures which minimise costs and which are based on internationally accepted classification rules and accounting principles. The other lesson is on how to prevent crises in the future. A country which wants to prevent future crises or minimise the losses when a crisis occurs should *reduce the vulnerability* of its economy by getting macroeconomic policies right and by ensuring sound banking, increasing international liquidity and shifting toward risk-based incentives in supervision regulations. To reduce the risk of financial contagion, it may be useful to *establish new multilateral economic institutions* with an aim of deepening economic cooperation within the region.

Using a unique microdata set, this study has analysed empirically the performance of the Thai banking industry, how it was affected by the crisis and the subsequent reforms and the effect of foreign bank entry on banking efficiency in Thailand after the significant acquisitions by foreign banks in 1999. With reference to cost efficiency, two main findings can be drawn from the bank-level panel data regressions. Firstly, the production costs of domestic and foreign banks are different, indicating that domestic and foreign banks are different in terms of business structures, management styles and customer bases. The foreign banks seemed to be more efficient than domestic banks in quality of bank management and risk and output quality (better capitalisation and lower levels of NPLs). On the other hand, domestic banks focused on liquidity of banks (high levels of liquid assets). Secondly, the unit costs of production of domestic and foreign banks are indistinguishable. Based on cost efficiency, foreign banks did not outperform domestic banks suggesting that if foreign banks represent the best-practice banks in the industry, to a large extent, domestic banks in Thailand have caught up to the best-practice standards throughout 1995-2003.

As for labour costs, loans and other earning assets are labour intensive. On average, the labour productivity of all types of banks is indifferent. During the post-crisis period, per unit labour costs of domestic banks are lowest, followed by foreign banks and merged banks. One possible explanation is that merged banks performed major downsizing and reorganisation in the early phase of acquisitions which incurred high costs, in particular the early retirement schemes. As for physical capital costs, foreign banks are less efficient in managing resale agreements and investment securities than domestic banks. In contrast, foreign banks are more efficient in managing loans than domestic banks resulting either from better monitoring systems and risk management or better loan quality in their portfolios. With reference to choice of input, the main findings are as follows; firstly, there are no significant differences in terms of labour shares among the three bank groups. Secondly, the labour cost shares of domestic and foreign banks declined during the post-crisis period. Thirdly, physical capital inputs of banks depend on banks' strategies which need long-term commitments.

In view of effects of foreign bank entry through acquisitions on cost efficiency, based on a domestic and merged (representing banks with more than 50 percent of foreign ownership since 1999) bank-level data set, the empirical results show two main findings. Firstly, per unit production costs of domestic banks are positively related to cash and inter-bank assets, loans and other earning assets; on the other hand, the costs of merged banks are negatively related to cash and inter-bank assets and other earning assets, indicating that domestic and merged banks have similar business structures as expected. Secondly, per unit production cost efficiency of domestic banks after the acquisition year declined, suggesting that the cost efficiency of domestic banks improved. One possible reason for this is that greater foreign bank participation through acquisition increases the competitive pressure in the banking industry, and also to financial restructuring of domestic banks, which increases the cost efficiency of domestic banks.

Recently, renewed consideration has been given to exploring the possible connection between the financial system and economic growth. This consideration stems from the on-going beliefs of applied economists and policy-makers that financial markets and institutions play important roles in the growth process. The study presents empirical work on the dynamic relationship between financial development and economic growth from a regional perspective. There are many cross-country studies relating to the relationship between growth and financial development; however, there is less evidence on the effect of local financial development within the regions of a single country. In fact, there are many advantages of examining the relationship between finance and growth in a regional perspective within a single country; for example, (1) the region/province represents a more accurate definition of the relevant retail bank market and (2) all related institutional, legal and cultural factors are likely to be constant across regions/provinces within a country, thereby ensuring that differences in economic performance across regions/provinces are not driven by those factors. This empirical study has two main objectives; to examine whether the financial development and the associated changes in the banking industry contributed to the economic performance and to investigate whether there is a causal relationship, and if so, in what direction it is running.

Based on pooled cross-province, time-series and purely cross province analyses, the main findings are as follows; (1) the growth rates of real gross provincial product (GPP) per capita for 23 years between 1981 and 2003 are significantly negatively related to the initial level of real GPP per capita (1981) as expected from absolute convergence in the growth theory. (2) Regarding the concept of conditional convergence, there is divergence of real GPP per capita/worker in Thailand during 1994-2003, suggesting that when taking financial development and other related variables into consideration, the richer provinces grew faster than the poorer ones. When the initial level of real GPP per capita/worker is held constant, neither credits nor branches robustly correlated with growth. One possible reason for this is that since the 1997 Thai financial crisis there is an increase in lending by important Specialised Financial Institutions (SFIs) at the provincial level like the Bank for Agriculture and Agricultural Co-operatives (BAAC), whose financial data are not included in this study. Despite of statistical insignificance, a possible explanation for the negative correlation between growth and credits is that those provinces which faced strong credit growth before the crisis (1994-1997) experienced a larger recession of GPP in 1997-1998 and a slower recovery thereafter. Based on the Granger causality test results, there is a bi-directional causality between finance and growth.

The following policy implications can be drawn from the preceding analysis:

(1) How to manage and prevent a crisis should be at the centre of policy makers concerns. As indicated in chapter 2, economic crises will probably continue to occur in the future as they have for centuries. Currency and banking crises are not a new episode. Crises seem to act like a hydra: whenever something has been learned from experience, new characteristics of a succeeding crisis emerge. However, once a crisis occurs, it is costly to both players within the financial systems and public finance. Lessons we learn from history provide knowledge about crises, both how to diagnose and how to manage and prevent them. According to an old western saying `an ounce of prevention is worth a pound of cure` which is similar to the old Thai saying `Kunwei-deekua-kae`. As the experience from the Thai financial crisis shows, this wisdom is not old fashion; it is always applicable. One of the main elements to prevent crises is an effective Early Warning System (EWS). Practically, effective EWSs in association with the experience of authorities' concerned and effective collaboration from the international community should try to prevent or at least minimise the cost of a crisis both in the affected country and in other countries whose economies are closely linked to the crisis country. The other element is strengthening the country's economy by creating a sound and stable macroeconomic environment and well-functioning and strong financial system. Another element is the availability of a dynamic and adaptive policy regime

(2) Financial Reform is a never-ending process and it needs long-term political commitments. Since the financial crisis in 1997 and joining the IMF package, Thailand has implemented an austerity policy programme, which includes comprehensive macroeconomic policy to restore stability both internally and externally. The programme includes financial reform. Many policy measures have been conducted in this respect and many policy measures are still on-going processes. In addition, the authorities concerned, like the central bank, also encourage financial institutions to strengthen themselves to face the dynamic global changes such as new financial products, innovations, information technology, cross-border competition and regulatory changes, for example, the new BIS Capital Accord (BOT, 2002). However, without long term political commitments, a threat to the success of the reform can emerge. For example, the Financial Institutions Businesses Act which will empower the Bank of Thailand to oversee and supervise financial institutions based on consolidated supervision and the establishment of a Deposit Insurance Agency to prevent the problem of moral hazard have not been finalised and need long term political commitments.

(3) Implementing best business practices including corporate governance can strengthen banks' competitiveness. The unit costs of production of domestic and foreign banks (representing banks with 100 percent of foreign ownership) are indistinguishable. Concerning foreign bank entry, domestic banks improved their cost efficiency since the acquisition by foreign banks in the Thai banking industry, illustrating that domestic banks have had to improve the quality of bank management to compete with the new players[1].

(4) More financial access may be a solution for promoting sustained growth. Empirical evidence from chapter 4 shows that there is a bi-directional causality between finance and growth in Thailand. However, according to the concept of conditional convergence, there is divergence of provincial growth in Thailand during 1994-2003, indicating that when taking financial development and other related variables into account, the richer provinces grew faster than the poorer ones. The authorities concerned should be aware of this trend and find out solutions for this drawback. One of the possible solutions is to increase access to finance for the poor provinces, and particularly for small entrepreneurs. This will increase overall investment, create more jobs in the areas and upgrade their living standards. In addition, improving the economic environment, including basic infrastructure should be a priority. Finally,

[1] The author's experience in involving in corporate debt workout after the 1997 crisis reveals that domestic banks who followed the best practice and regulations in doing their business as well as engaged in restructuring could survive from the crisis and return to profitability, indicating that it is possible for Thai banks to compete with the foreign banks in the Thai financial market.

promoting sustained economic growth in a changing and complex financial environment is a difficult task but it is worthwhile.

References

Agenor, Pierre-Richard (2001), Benefits and Costs of International Financial Integration: Theory and Facts, *World Bank Policy Research Working Paper*, 2699, November.

Alba, Pedro, Leonardo Hernandez and Daniela Klingebiel (1999), Financial Liberalisation and the Capital Account: Thailand 1988-1997, *World Bank Policy Research Working Paper*, 2188, September.

Allen, Franklin (2003), Financial Crises: Part II: Historical and Recent Crises, Course Materials, Bendheim Center for Finance, Economic Department, Princeton University, Spring Semester 2003 (http://finance.wharton.upenn.edu/allenf/).

Allen, Franklin and Douglas Gale (2003), Understanding Financial Crises, Calrendon Lectures in Finance, University of Pennsylvania, June 9-11, 2003 (http://finance.wharton.upenn.edu/allenf/).

Anderson, T. and C. Hsiao (1981), Estimation of Dynamic Models with Error Components, *Journal of the American Statistical Association*, 78, 598-606.

Anderson, T. and C. Hsiao (1982), Formulation and Estimation of Dynamic Models Using Panel Data, *Journal of Econometrics*, 18, 47-82.

Arellano, M. and O. Bover (1995), Another Look at the IV Estimation of Error Components Model, *Journal of Econometrics*, 68, 29-62.

Arellano, Manuel and Stephen Bond, (1991), Some Tests of Specification for Panel Data: Monte Carlo Evidence and an Application to Employment Equations, *Review of Economic Studies*, 58(2), 277-297 (April).

Arteta, Carlos and Barry, Eichengreen (2000), Banking Crises in Emerging Markets: Presumptions and Evidence, Working Paper C00-115, Centre for International and Development Economic Research (CIDER), University of California at Berkeley.

Babson, Oliver D. and Steven B. Kamin (1999), The Contribution of Domestic and External Factors to Latin American Devaluation Crises: An Early Warning Systems Approach, Board of Governors of the Federal Reserve System, *International Finance Discussion Paper*, 645, September.

Bäckström, Urban (1997), What Lessons can be Learned from Recent Financial Crises?: The Swedish Experience, Symposium Proceedings 'Managing Financial Stability in Global Economy', sponsored by the Federal Reserve Bank of Kansas City, Jackson Hole, Wyoming, August 28-30.

Baltagi, Badi H. (1995), Econometric Analysis of Panel Data, John Wiley & Sons.

Bank for International Settlements (BIS) (1999), *Policy Papers*, 6 –Bank Restructuring in Practice, August.

Bank of Thailand (1999), Annual Report.

Bank of Thailand (2000), Annual Report.

Bank of Thailand (2001), Supervision Report 2000.

Bank of Thailand (2003), Supervision Report 2001-2002.

Bank of Thailand (2004), The Financial Sector Master Plan, Bank of Thailand News, No. 1/2004, January.

Barro, J. Robert and Xavier Sala-i-Martin (1998), Economic Growth, MIT Press.

Barro, Robert J., (2001), Economic Growth in East Asian before and after the Financial Crises, *NBER Working Paper*, 8330, June.

Beck, Thorsten Ross Levine and Norman Loayza (2000a), Finance and the Sources of Growth, *Journal of Financial Economics*, 58, 261-300.

Beck, Thorsten, Asli Demirguc-Kunt, Ross Levine and Vojislav Maksimovic (2000b), Financial Structure and Economic Development: Firm, Industry and Country Evidence, *World Bank Policy Research Working Paper*, 2423, (June).

Beckmann, Daniela and Lukas Menkhoff (2004), Early Warning Systems: Lessons from New Approaches, in Michael Frenkel, Alexander Karmann and Bert Scholtens (Eds.), Sovereign Risk, Financial Crises and Stability, Springer, Berlin.

Bencivenga, Valerie R. and Bruce D. Smith, (1991), Financial Intermediation and Endogenous Growth, *The Review of Economic Studies*, 58(2), 195-209 (April).

Berger, Allen N. and David B. Hamphrey (1997), Efficiency of Financial Institutions: International Survey and Directions for Future Research, *Working Paper*, No. 97-05, The Wharton Financial Institutions Centre, The Wharton School, University of Pennsylvania.

Berger, Allen N. and Loretta J. Mester (1997), Inside the Black Box: What Explains Differences in the Efficiencies of Financial Institutions?, *Journal of Banking and Finance*, 21(7), 895-1063.

Berger, Allen N. Iftekhar Hasan and Leora F. Klapper (2004), Further Evidence on the Link between Finance and Growth: An International Analysis of Community Banking and Economic Performance, *Journal of Financial Services Research*, 25(2/3), 169-202.

Bergsten, C. Fred (2000), The New Asian Challenge, *Working Paper*, 00-4, Institute for International Economics (IIE), March.

Bhagwati, Jagdish N. (2002). The Wind of the Hundred Days: How Washington Mismanaged Globalization, The MIT Press, Cambridge, Massachusetts, London

Blundell, R. and S. Bond (1998), Initial Conditions and Moment Restrictions in Dynamic Panel Data Models, Journal of Econometrics, 87 (1), 115-143.

Bordo, Michael and Anna J. Schwartz (1996), Why Clashes between Internal and External Stability Goals End in Currency Crises, 1797-1994, *NBER Working Paper*, 5710, August.

Bordo, Michael and Anna J. Schwartz (2000), Measuring Real Economic Effects of Bailouts: Historical Perspectives on How Countries in Financial Distress Have Fared with and Without Bailouts, *NBER Working Paper*, 7701, May.

Bordo, Michael and Barry Eichengreen (2002), Crises Now and Then: What Lessons from the Last Era of Financial Globalisation?, *NBER Working Paper*, 8716, January.

Buch, C. M. and Ralph P. Heinrich (1999), Twin Crises and the Intermediary Role of Banks, *International Journal of Financial and Economics*, 4, 313-323.

Calvo, Guillermo and Carmen M. Reinhart (2000), Fear of Floating, *NBER Working Paper*, 7993, November.

Caprio, G. and Daniela Klingebiel (1996), Bank Insolvencies: Cross Country Experience, *World Bank Policy Research Working Paper,* 1620, July.

Caprio, Gerard and Dimitri Vittas, (1995), Financial History: Lessons of the Past for Reformers of the Present, *World Bank Policy Research Working Paper*, 1535, November.

Casu, Barbara Claudia Girardone and Philip Molyneux (2004), Productivity Change in European Banking: A Comparison of Parametric and Non-parametric Approaches, *Journal of Banking and Finance*, 28(10), 2521-2540.

Christensen, Björn (2001), Applied Econometrics I (second draft), Notes for the Advanced Studies Programme in International Economic Policy Research 2001/2002, the Kiel Institute of World Economics, Kiel, Germany.

Claessens, Stijn and Luc Laeven (2003), What Drives Bank Competition? Some International Evidence, *World Bank Policy Research Working Paper*, 3113, August.

Claessens, Stijn (1999), Systemic Bank Restructuring: Experiences and Lessons, Paper Presented at Seminar: Managing Capital Flows in a Volatile Financial Environment, Bangkok, Thailand, February 22-25.

Claessens, Stijn Asli Demirguc-Kunt and Harry Huizinga (2000), The Role of Foreign Banks in Domestic Banking Systems in Claessens S. and Jansen M. (eds), The Internationalization of Financial Services, Kluwer Law International, Great Britain.

Claessens, Stijn Asli Demirguc-Kunt and Harry Huizinga (2001), How does Foreign Entry Affect Domestic Banking Markets?, *Journal of Banking and Finance*, 25(5), 891-911.

Claessens, Stijn Daniela Klingebiel and Luc Laeven (2001), Financial Restructuring in Systemic Crises: What Policies to Pursue?, *NBER Working Paper,* 8386, July.

Claessens, Stijn Daniela Klingebiel and Luc Laeven (2004), Resolving Systemic Financial Crises: Policies and Institutions, *World Bank Policy Research Working Pape,* 3377, August.

Clarke, George Robert Cull Maria Soledad Martinez Peria and Susana M. Sanchez (2001), Foreign Bank Entry: Experience, Implications for Developing Countries, and Agenda for Further Research, *World Bank Policy Research Working Paper*, 2698, October.

Corsetti, Giancarlo Paolo Pesenti and Nouriel, Roubini (1998a), What caused the Asian Currency and Financial Crisis? Part I: A Macroeconomic Overview, *NBER Working Paper*, 6833, December.

Corsetti, Giancarlo Paolo Pesenti and Nouriel Roubini (1998b), What caused the Asian Currency and Financial Crisis? Part II: The Policy Debate, *NBER Working Paper*, 6834, December.

Corsetti, Giancarlo Paolo Pesenti and Nouriel Roubini (1998c), Fundamental Determinants of the Asian Crisis: A Preliminary Empirical Assessment, Paper presented to the JIMF-Fordham University Conference on 'Perspectives on the Financial Crises in Asia, November.

Corsetti, Giancarlo Paolo Pesenti and Nouriel Roubini (2001a), Fundamental Determinants of the Asian Crisis: the Role of Financial Fragility and External Imbalances, in Takatoshi Ito and Anne O. Krueger (eds.), Regional and Global Capital Flows: Macroeconomic Causes and Consequences, NBER-East Asia Seminar on Economics Vol. 20, 11-41, Chicago, IL: University of Chicago Press.

Corsetti, Giancarlo Paolo Pensenti, and Nouriel, Roubini (2001b), The Role of Large Players in Currency Crises, *NBER Working Paper*, 8303.

Crystal, Jennifer S. B. Gerard Degas and Linda S. Goldberg (2001), Does Foreign Ownership Contribute to Sounder Banks in Emerging Markets? The Latin American Experience, *Federal Reserve Bank of New York Staff Reports 134*, September.

Demetriades, P. and S. Andrianova (2003), Finance and Growth: What We Know and What We Need to Know, *Discussion Papers in Economics (DP03-15)*, Department of Economics, University of Leicester (October).

Demetriades, Panicos O. Michael P. Devereux and Kul B. Luintel (1998), Productivity and Financial Sector Policies: Evidence from South East Asia, *Journal of Economic Behavior & Organization*, 35, 61-82.

Detragiache, Enrica and Poonam Gupta (2004), Foreign Banks in Emerging Market Crises: Evidence from Malaysia, *IMF Working Paper*, WP/04/129, July.

Disyatat, Piti and Don Nakornthab (2003), The Changing Nature of Financial Structure in Thailand and Implications for Policy, *Bank of Thailand (BOT) Discussion Paper*, DP/06/2003, November.

Disyatat, Piti and Pinnarat Vongsinsirikul (2003), Monetary Policy and the Transmission Mechanism in Thailand, *Journal of Asian Economics*, 14(3), 389-418.

Durlauf, S. and P. Johnson (1995), Multiple Regimes and Cross-country Growth Behavior, *Journal of Applied Econometrics*, 10, 365-384.

Dziobek, Claudia and Pazarbasioglu Ceyla, (1998), Lessons from Systemic Bank Restructuring, *Economic Issue 14*, International Monetary Fund

Edison, Hali, (2000), Do Indicators of Financial Crises Work? An Evaluation of an Early Warning System, Board of Governors of the Federal Reserve System, *International Finance Discussion Paper*, 675, July.

Eichengreen, Barry and Richard Portes (1997), Managing Financial Crises in Emerging Markets, Symposium Proceedings 'Managing Financial Stability in Global Economy', sponsored by the Federal Reserve Bank of Kansas City, Jackson Hole, Wyoming, August 28-30.

Eichengreen, Barry Kenneth Kletzer and Ashoka Mody (2003), Crisis Resolution: Next Steps, *IMF Working Paper*, No. 03/196, October.

Ergungor, O. Emre (2003), Financial System Structure and Economic Development: Structure Matters, *Working Paper*, 0305, The Federal Reserve Bank of Cleveland.

Feldstein, Martin (1999), Self-Protection for Emerging Market Economies, *NBER Working Paper*, 6907, January.

Feldstein, Martin, (2000), Aspects of Global Economic Integration: Outlook for the Future, *NBER Working Paper*, 7899, September.

Feldstein, Martin (2002), Economic and Financial Crises in Emerging Markets Economies: Overview of Prevention and Management, *NBER Working Paper*, 8837, March.

Fohlin, Caroline (2000), Banking Industry Structure, Competition, and Performance: Does Universality Matter?, *Social Science Working Paper*, 1078, California Institute of Technology, October.

Fries, Steven and Anita Taci (2005), Cost Efficiency of Banks in Transition: Evidence from 289 Banks in 15 Post-communist Countries, *Journal of Banking and Finance*, 29(1), 55-81.

Gertler, Mark (1988), Financial Structure and Aggregate Economic Activity: An Overview, NBER Working Paper, 2559, (April).

Glick, Reuven and Michael Hutchison (1999), Banking and Currency Crises: How Common are Twins?, *Pacific Basin Working Paper Series*, No.PB99-07, Center for Pacific Basin Monetary and Economic Studies, Economic Research Department, Federal Reserve Bank of San Francisco

Goldberg, Linda B. Gerard Dages and Daniel Kinney (2000), Foreign and Domestic Bank Participation in Emerging Markets: Lessons from Mexico and Argentina, *NBER Working Paper*, 7714, May.

Grier, Robin (2003), Toothless Tiger? East Asian Economic Growth from 1960 to 1990, *Review of Development Economics,* 7(3), 392-405.

Guiso, Luigi Paola Sapienza and Luigi Zingales (2004), Does Local Financial Development Matter?, *The Quarterly Journal of Economics*, 119(3), 929-969.

Hall, Bronwyn H. Jacques Mairesse Lee Branstetter and Bruno Crepon (1998), Does Cash Flow Cause Investment and R&D?: An Exploration Using Panel Data for French, Japanese, and United States Scientific Firms, IFS Paper No. W98/11; *Nuffield College Paper*, 142 and *Berkeley Dept. of Economics Paper*, 98-260.

Hawkins, John (1999), Bank Restructuring in South-East Asia, *Policy Papers* , 6: Bank Restructuring in Practice, Bank for International Settlements (BIS), August.

Herberholz, Chantal (2002), The Impact of Foreign Entry on the Thai Domestic Banking Sector, Chulalongkorn Journal of Economics, 14(2), 178-214.

Hoggarth, Glenn Jack Reidhill and Peter Sinclair (2004), On the Resolution of Banking Crises: Theory and Evidence, *Bank of England Working Paper*, 229.

Hölscher, Jens (2000), Cantral Banking and Financial Stability in Transition Economies, in Alexander Karmann (ed), Financial Structure and Stability, Physica-Verlag: A Springer-Verlag.

Hsiao, Cheng (1986), Analysis of Panel Data, Econometric Society Monographs, 11, Cambridge University Press.

Hurlin, Christophe and Baptiste Venet (2001), Granger Causality Tests in Panel Data Models with Fixed Coefficients, *Cahier de Vecherche*, 2001-09, Centre de recherché EURisco, Universite Paris Dauphine, July.

Ingves, Stefan (2003), Banking Crisis from an International Perspective, Speech given at the Seminar on Financial Safety Nets, SEDESA (Seguro de Depósitos Sociedad Anónima) Buenos Aires, 8 April.

Intarachote, Thida and Jonathan Williams (2003), Financial Liberalisation and Profit Efficiency in the Thai Banking System, 1990-1997: the Case of Domestic and Foreign Banks, *SBARD (The School of Business and Regional Development) Research Papers*, University of Wales, Bangor, U.K.

International Monetary Fund (2002), Thailand: Selected Issues and Statistical Appendix, *IMF Country Report*, No. 02/195, September.

International Monetary Fund (2004), Thailand: Selected Issues, *IMF Country Report*, No. 04/1, January.

International Monetary Fund and the World Bank (2003), Analytical Tools of the Financial Sector Assessment Program (FSAP), (unpublished document), February.

International Monetary Fund and the World Bank (2003), Financial Sector Assessment Program – Review, Lessons and Issues Going Forward, (unpublished document), February.

International Monetary Fund, (2003), Thailand: Statistical Appendix, IMF Country Report No. 03/388, December.

Islam, Nazrul (1999), International Comparison of Total Factor Productivity: A Review, Review of Income and Wealth, Series 45, No.4, 493-518 , December.

Jayaratne, Jith Philip E. Strahan (1996), The Finance-Growth Nexus: Evidence from Bank Branch Dereguation, The Quarterly Journal of Economics, 111(3), 639-670, August.

Jehle, Geoffrey A. and Philip J. Reny (2001), *Advanced Microeconomic Theory: Second edition*, Addison Wesley.

Johnston, Jack and John DiNardo (1997), *Econometric Methods: fourth edition*, The McGraw-Hill Companies, Inc.

Kaminsky, Graciela L. and Carmen M. Reinhart (1999), The Twin Crises: The Causes of Banking and Balance-of-Payments Problems, *American Economic Review*, 89(3), 473-500.

Kaminsky, Graciela L. (1998), Currency and Banking Crises: The Early Warnings of Distress, *International Finance Discussion Paper*, 629, Board of Governors of the Federal Reserve System, October.

Kaminsky, Graciela L. and Carmen Reinhart (2003), The Centre and the Periphery: The Globalisation of Financial Turmoil, NBER Working Paper , 9479, January.

Kawai, Masahiro Richard Newfarmer and Sergio Schmukler (2001), Crisis and Contagion in East Asia: Nine Lessons, *World Bank Policy Research Working Paper*, 2610, February.

Kim, Taeho (1993), *International Money and Banking*, Routledge, London and New York.

King, Robert G. and Ross Levine (1993), Finance and Growth: Schumpeter Might be Right, *The Quarterly Journal of Economics*, 108(3), 717-737.

Klump, Rainer, (2003), Was Growth Pro-poor in Vietnam? --Assessment and Policy Recommendation--, Deutsche Gesellschaft für Technische Zusammenarbeit (GTZ).

Krugman, Paul (2000), Crises: The Price of Globalisation? in Global Economic Integration: Opportunities and Challenges Symposium, sponsored by The Federal Reserve Bank of Kansas City, 75-106.

Krugman, Pual, (1999), Balance Sheet, the Transfer Problem, and Financial Crises, International Tax and Public Finance, 6, pp. 459-472

Kwan, Simon H. (2003), Operating Performance of Banks among Asian Economies: an International and Times Series Comparison, *Journal of Banking and Finance*, 27(3), 471-489.

Lamfaussy, Aleandre (2000) "Financial Crises in Emerging Markets: An Essay on Financial Globalisation and Fragility", Yale University Press, New Haven & London.

Leightner, Jonathan E. and C.A. Knox Lovell (1998), The Impact of Financial Liberalisation on the Performance of Thai Banks, *Journal of Economics and Business*, 50(2), 115-131.

Levine, Ross Norman Loayza and Thorsten Beck (2000), Financial Intermediation and Growth: Causality and Causes, *Journal of Monetary Economics*, 46, 31-77.

Maggi, Bernardo and Stefania P.S. Rossi (2003), An Efficiency Analysis of Banking Systems: A Comparison of European and United States Large Commercial Banks using Different Functional Forms, *Working Paper*, 03-35, European Integration, Financial Systems and Corporate Performance (EIFC) Consortium, the United Nations University, Institute for New Technologies, Maastricht.

Mahajan, Arvind Nanda Rangan and Asghar Zardkoohi (1996), Cost Structure in Multinational and Domestic Banking, *Journal of Banking and Finance*, 20(2), 283-306.

Majnoni, Giovanni Rashmi Shankar and Eva Varhegyi (2003), The Dynamic of Foreign Bank Ownership: Evidence from Hungary, *World Bank Policy Research Working Paper*, 3114, August.

McDonough, William J. (2003), Promoting Financial Resilience, *The Cato Journal*, 23 (1):11-21 (Spring/Summer 2003), Public Company Accounting Oversight Board, Washington, D.C.

Menkhoff, Lukas and Chodechai Suwanaporn (2003), The Rationale of Bank Lending in Pre-Crisis Thailand, Discussion Papers on Development Policy, ZEF (Zentrum für Entwicklungsforschung) Center for Development Research, Bonn, August.

Menkhoff, Lukas (2000), Bad Banking in Thailand? An Empirical Analysis of Macro Indicators, *Journal of Development Studies*, 36, 135-168

Mester, Loretta J. (1996), A Study of Bank Efficiency taking into Account Risk-preferences, *Journal of Banking and Finance*, 20(6), 1025-1045.

Mishkin, Frederic S. (2000), Financial Policies and the Prevention of Financial Crises in Emerging Market Countries, prepared for NBER Conference, Economic and Financial Crises in Emerging Markets Countries, Woodstock, Vermont, October 19-21.

Molnar, Margit (2003), Post-Crisis Changes in Banking and Corporate Landscapes- The Case of Thailand, *Economics Department Working Paper*, 363, Organisation for Economic Co-operation and Development (OECD), July.

Mori, Nobuhiro and Yoshiro Tsutsui (1993), The Industrial Organisation of Financial Markets in Thailand, *Asian Economic Journal*, 7(1), 71-88.

Obstfeld, Maurice (1994), The Logic of Currency Crises, *NBER Working Paper*, 4640, September.

Pensenti, Paolo and Cedric Tille (2000), The Economics of Currency Crises and Contagion: An Introduction, *Federal Reserve Bank of New York (FRBNY) Economic Policy Review*, 6(3), September.

Prasad, Eswar Kenneth Rogoff Shang-Jin Wei and Ayhan Kose (2003), Effects of Financial Globalisation on Developing Countries: Some Empirical Evidence, *IMF Occasional Paper*, 220, September.

Radelet, Steven and Jeffrey Sachs (1998), The onset of the East Asian Financial Crisis, NBER Working Paper, 6680, August.

Rahman, Shahidur Lian Hwa Tan Ooi Lyn Hew and Yih San Tan (2004), Identifying Financial Distress Indicators of Selected Banks in Asia, *Asian Economic Journal*, 18(1), 45-57.

Rousseau, Peter L. and Richard Sylla (2001), Financial Systems, Economic Growth, and Globalisation, *NBER Working Paper*, 8323, June.

Rousseau, Peter L. (2003), Historical Perspectives on Financial Development and Economic Growth, *The Federal Reserve Bank of St. Louis Review*, 85(4), 81-106 (July/August).

Rouvinen, Petri (2002), R&D-Productivity Dynamics: Causality, Lags, and 'Dry Holes', *Journal of Applied Economics*, V(1), 123-156, May.

Sabi, Manijeh (1996), Comparative Analysis of Foreign and Domestic Bank Operations in Hungary, *Journal of Comparative Economics*, 22(2), 179-188.

Saqib, Omar F. (2002), Interpreting Currency Crises- A Review of Theory, Evidence, and Issues, DIW Berlin, German Institute for Economic Research, October.

Senivongs na Ayudhya, Chirathep Pornvipa Tangcharoenmonkong and Thitima Chucherd (2003), Balance Sheets and Economic Recovery, paper presented in Bank of Thailand Symposium 2003, August.

Sirivedhin, Tanya (1998), Financial Reform and the Monetary Transmission Mechanism: The Case of Thailand, *BIS Policy Paper*, 3, 195-222, January.

Stata User's Guide Release 8 (2003), A Stata Press Publication, Stata Corporation, College Station, Texas

Stone, Mark R. (2002), Corporate Sector Restructuring: The Role of Government in Times of Crisis, *IMF Economic Issues*, 31, June.

Sturm, Jan-Egbert and Barry Williams (2004), Foreign Bank Entry, Deregulation and Bank Efficiency: Lessons from the Australia Experience, *Journal of Banking and Finance*, 28(7), 1775-1799.

Timmer, Marcel P. (2001), Financial and Economic Crises in Asia, Review of the Asian Financial Crisis: Causes, Contagion and Consequences, in Pierre-Richard Agenor, Marcus Miller, David Vines and Axel Weber (eds), and The Indonesian Economy in Crisis: Causes, Consequences and Lessons by Hal Hill (1999), Review of Income and Wealth, 47(1), 125-133, March.

Valverde, Santiago Carbo and Francisco Rodriguez Fernandez (2004), The Finance-Growth Nexus: A Regional Perspective, *European Urban and Regional Studies*, 11 (4), 339-354.

Valverde, Santiago Carbo, Rafael Lopez del Paso and Francisco Rodriguez Fernandez (2004), Banks, Financial Innovations and Regional Growth (Project Financed by the European Commission, DG Research- Improving the Human Potential and the Socio-Economic Knowledge Base Programme), *Working Paper*, 04-34, the United Nations University, The Netherlands (June).

Wallich, Henry C. (1969), Uses of Financial Accounts in Monetary Analysis, *The Review of Income and Wealth*, Series 15, 321-334.

Weller, Christian (1999), Financial Liberalisation, Multinational Banks and Credit Supply: The Case of Poland, *Working Paper*, B10, Centre for European Integration Studies, Rheinische Friedrich-Wilhelms-Universitat Bonn.

Williamson, John (1999), Implications of the East Asia Crisis for Debt Management, paper presented to a conference on 'External Debt Management', organised by the Reserve Bank of India, the Indian Ministry of Finance and the World Bank, Koyalam, Kerala, January 7-9.

World Bank (1993), The East Asian Miracle: Economic Growth and Public Policy, Oxford et al.: Oxford University Press

World Bank (1997), Private Capital Flows to Developing Countries, Washington, D.C.

Kolibri 360 GmbH
Ferdinand-Jühlke-Straße 7
99095 Erfurt, Deutschland
produktsicherheit@kolibri360.de

Druck:
CPI Druckdienstleistungen GmbH
im Auftrag der
Kolibri 360 GmbH
Ferdinand-Jühlke-Str. 7
99095 Erfurt